OCIOLOGY FOR BEGINNERS

Plea
Dych

First published in the UK by Icon books Ltd. In 1996
Reprinted in 1997, 1998, 2000, 2002, 2004, 2005, 2009

This edition first published by Zidane Books 2015

Copyright @ Zidanepress Ltd.

Text @ Richard Osborne
Final design and layout by Michaela Stasova

Updated edition 2016 copyright Richard Osborne

Distributed by:

Turnaround Publisher Services Ltd.
Unit 3, Olympia Trading Estate
London, N 22 6TZ
Ph. (0)208 829 3000
www.turnaround-uk.com

British Library Catalogue in publication data.

ISBN. 978-0956267870

SO YOU WANT TO BE A SOCIOLOGIST?

Well the first thing you need is imagination.

Think hard and imagine yourself as a Siberian coal miner working in minus 20c temperatures and not being paid for six months.

What would be your reaction to this and to the break-up of the old Communist Soviet Union?

If you can imagine what it is like to live on boiled potatoes and cabbage for six months, not be paid and not even be able to go online, then you've probably got a sociological imagination and you're half-way there.

The other half is some idea about how people function in groups and some idea about how to do research.

Sociology is basically about thinking about how people live in society.

Sociology is also like learning to ride a bike, once you've done it, it seems obvious but try explaining it to someone else.

What sociologists attempt to do is explain the different forces and influences that shape how someone grows up, or is 'socialized'.

The ability to look at society like an alien would help as well.

What would ET have made of snow boarding, for example?

Whether communism was a good thing is a very interesting sociological question and one that does need some imagination, and some history.

The main reason it is an interesting question is because communism was an attempt to completely rebuild society - which is what sociology is rather interested in. In a way, communism was supposed to be sociology applied to restructuring society.

The debate about how much one can reshape society is rather central to the sociological project. The problem of sociology is understanding why society functions at all, and why people accept society's control.

Where did sociology come from, you ask?

Well, sociology is a very modern science, so modern in fact that a lot of right-wing neo-liberals say that it isn't a science, or anything else at all.

Mrs Thatcher was very fond of saying that "there is no such thing as society", and since that is what sociologists study you can see that she doesn't think much of sociology.

Sociologists, on the other hand, often say that sociology is the science of society and the route to curing all known social problems.

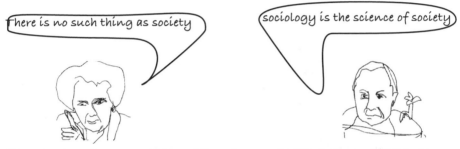

So nobody agrees on what sociology is, on what it studies, what it is for and if people should do it. However society clearly exists, and changes, so it must be possible to study it in some way.

If you believed that individuals could do whatever they liked, you would ultimately have to approve of any sort of human behaviour, including murder.

WHAT IS SOCIOLOGY?

It's what left-wingers do at college in between drinking too much and demonstrating.

It's a long word, man.

or it's a way of explaining how society throws up people like you

AC: It's something I invented in the bath in the 1820's and it means a new way of thinking about society and how it can change, and develop. I was the first to use the word and I am positive that it will be a great benefit to everybody.

It is the broadest and most complicated of human sciences which draws on all the others. It is about everything that human beings do in social inter-action, which is just about everything.

Auguste Comte

If you want to do sociology its probably because you are interested in the society you live in and how it works.

We are all aware that the societies we now live in are changing rapidly and that the world our parents knew has probably dissappeared for good.

Change makes some people very unhappy and others think its wonderful.

Do people make society change or is it technology?

That is a typical sort of sociological question.

How individuals live in the digital age is another important question.

The idea of sociology grew out of a realization that societies do change, beginning in the modern era with the French and American Revolutions.

In the 18th & 19th centuries America and Europe changed from being agricultural societies into industrial societies and this was a very major shift, the consequences of which we are still living through.

Sociology is a way of sitting back from all the development and asking, "What caused that to happen" and "Why do people do things like that?"

Aristotle

As an example take a look at judges, who have been around in different forms for a very long time. When they are locking people up judges often say "You are a danger to society" or "society must be protected from people like you".

Now if Mrs Thatcher was right and society doesn't exist then people obviously shouldn't be locked up for being a danger to it. Either the judges or Mrs Thatcher have got it completely wrong. In fact if society didn't exist then judges would not have a job, or any authority or reason to lock people up.

The law is of course an important part of society that governs how things run, or are supposed to run.

So sociology wants to say, " how do these things work?" Why do judges make the decisions they do, how do prisons work and why do people commit crimes? Is it because they are bad, hungry or because they saw it on television?"

In Britain and America the question of racial equality is still a big one in society, and racism is an important sociological issue.

You might have noticed that any kind of talking about society immediately gets into problems about whose definition you are using.

The judge assumes that his definition of things is always right and that anybody who disagrees is a trouble-maker.

Because people assume certain things are just common-sense, like judges' rights to lock people up, it means that sociology often has to confront common sense.

This leads to big arguments about opinion, history, the way things ought to be, the way things were and how to put them right.

In other words society isn't a fixed, static thing that you can put under the microscope and examine like a fossil or an amoeba This may seem obvious but in fact some sociologists have, in the past, got carried away with looking at society as though it were a natural, organic thing that could be explained like plant life or bee hives.

The question is whether you can examine society in a scientific way.

THE PROBLEM OF IDEOLOGY

Is it a hernia?

INDIVIDUAL PROBLEMS — WIDER SOCIOLOGICAL STRUCTURES

The problem is that as soon as you talk about people you end up talking about society, and whenever you try and explain how society works you have to talk about people.

This is just to say that the real difference with trying to talk about society is that people act, think and behave in very complicated ways that are completely unlike animals, machines or chemicals.

What makes people different is that they think and change the ways they behave, so you have to consider first of all how people think. People's minds are what makes them different to animals. The fact that people believe in society also differentiates them from animals.

The other very important point is that people basically function in groups, they do very little on their own and depend on other people for all kinds of support.

So there is a real conundrum in the idea of sociology.

The reason that sociology is important is that without knowledge of how our societies work, or don't work, it is impossible to frame policies about anything. Governments have to have some idea of what effects their actions might have, otherwise they would be planning things in the dark. (Many governments appear to do just this.)

That's the meta-level. At a personal level you never know who you are until you realise what made you they way you are.

It's the social and the personal combined that really makes sociology an interesting subject. Some disciplines just deal with one little bit of human behaviour, like chiropody, that deals with your feet, but sociology tries to look at the big picture and see how it all fits together.

Understanding social forces and the effect they have on a particular individual is what makes sociology so interesting and complex. We know that society changes and so we really want to know what it might change into. So there is historical sociology which wants to look at the past, and futurology that wants to look at the future.

A good example of why sociology is important is when someone from another country comes here (Britain) as a refugee. Often they don't know the language or, more importantly, the customs, and so they don't have a clue what's going on. To adapt they have to try and understand how a different culture operates. A good sociological approach could tell you how the refugee reacts and how the host society also reacts. Then it ought to be possible for both to co-exist.

If you look at Australians and Americans who go to Britain it's even clearer because they speak the same language, or they appear to, but their idea of how things work is often very different. Australians are very open and friendly, mostly, but the English are often very shy and reserved.

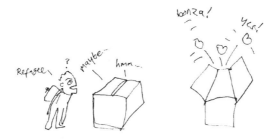

Language is very important here in communicating different understandings.

The present issue of refugees poses a very difficult question for modern societies, and how to deal with them has become a very big issue.

So what is Society?

It is the rules and patterns and laws that make up the way people live together, often in ways that have developed throughout the modern, industrial era.

We have capitalist society, the free-market, some communist societies, some, like China, that are now a mixture of both, and democratic societies and authoritarian societies, and they all have different ways of organising things.

If you look around you see people behaving in an everyday way doing things that seem natural, like taking the dog for a walk, but why they do it in a particular way is an interesting sociological question.

In present day society everyone has a great deal of choice, that is what is meant by a 'free-society" and providing choice is what most governments aspire to do. We can choose our identity, our image, our activities and, some people argue, our bodies- through diet, exercise and even plastic surgery.
The internet has transformed modern society in the last twenty years and appears to offer unlimited choice of everything, so is this a completely different form of society?

The individual is seen as key in contemporary society, and individual choice is worshipped almost as a religion, but the sociological question is: "How much choice do people really have?"

Why do some people conform to the dominant culture and why do some people rebel and reject the way society is organised?

Again in contemporary society the question of terrorism has become a very important issue. Why do some people reject ordinary society so completely that they want to try and destroy it and replace it with something else? These difficult questions are what sociology tries to deal with.

Centrally we could say that the question is how does contemporary society shape the individual and the ways in which they react to society's rules?

Other tricky questions that sociology has to try and deal with are:

How does education work in the digital age?

Are we all changing because of the globalised world economy?

Here is a question that neatly frames some of the dilemmas of sociology.

Why am I unemployed?

There is mass unemployment in modern societies and people who lose their jobs often feel at fault, that they have failed in some way. Importantly they tend to think of the problem in an individual way. Again this is a common-sense view but there are obviously wider and more complicated issues why people might end up unemployed.

Sociology as a discipline would try to analyse all of the factors, both social and individual, that led to unemployment. If you think about work skills as well, they have to come from somewhere - an individual doesn't invent them.

Surplus Labour

The real reasons for unemployment could actually be:

1) Technological changes
(computers and robots replacing labour)
2) Improved working practices (efficiency/technology)
3) Jobs moving to other countries (globilization)
4) Political changes (government policy)
5) Cultural change (different products wanted)
6) Lack of relevant skills (the digital age)
7) No access to re-training/education

None of these factors have anything to do with
individual input, but are wider social patterns.

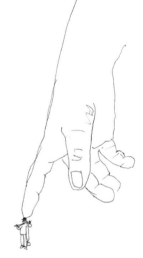

Thus, an individual viewpoint is mostly irrelevant in assessing the underlying cause of unemployment. One out of ten thousand might be made redundant because of laziness, but the rest are surplus because society has changed. But blaming the individual is a common political practice.

Some societies have tried to react to these changes in the global economy but many individuals are badly affected by these sweeping changes.

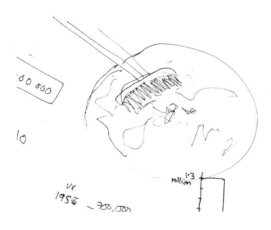

Industrial change

In the last twenty years the way in which industrial societies have been organised has been totally transformed.

In the 18th and 19th centuries America and Europe changed from being agricultural societies into industrial ones. This was a very major shift, the consequences of which we are still living through. Now in the West all of the old heavy industries, like steel, coal and ship building, have declined rapidly and have been moved to the emerging, developing new countries, like China, India, Korea, Brazil, etc. So thousands of jobs in these old industries have disappeared in the Western ,advanced economies.
In a globilised economy jobs migrate from the expensive advanced economies to places where labour costs are cheaper, which has led to the disappearance of millions of jobs in the old, richer countries. In Britain for example almost every single coal mining job has disappeared. There were once 1.3 million coal mining jobs there are now about 100.

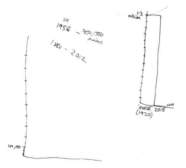

Understanding these changes and how they impact on people is a central theme of sociology. It was the industrial revolution and the impact it began to have on society that kicked sociology off. The French and American Revolutions also gave birth to the modern era, an era of constant change.

How unemployed people see themselves as to blame for their unemployment brings us to the question of Ideology.

What is ideology?

This key concept in sociology relates to how people absorb and believe in dominant ideas that give a false picture of the world.

Individualism is a key ideology in Western societies, the idea that the individual is the centre and focus of everything that occurs, that a free individual can simply choose to be employed or unemployed. If there are no jobs then what an individual does has no impact, and to blame themselves is an ideological response.

Ideology often presents a 'common-sense' view of the world, that the individual is responsible for everything. This question of common-sense and the inability to link individual problems to wider sociological structures is precisely what we mean by the problem of ideology.

My friends, I stand for blind prejudice and commonsense ideology.

Sociology threatens ordinary understanding of how things work, and that is why it irritates many people.

False consciousness

The word ideology has many meanings but they all tend to describe how people believe certain things about the world that may not be true. Common sense ideas about the world are frequently ideological, in the sense that they are beliefs rather than scientific description.

The belief that black people are less intelligent and genetically different to white people is an ideology. It is not a a scientifically justified set of ideas. Many of the views that people hold about society, and how things should work, like marriage or schooling, are based on ideologies rather than abstract thought about culture and social behaviour.

> I describe ideology as false consciousness, by which I mean people believe things that are untrue, and which delude them about their real social position.

Many workers used to believe that the upper classes had a right to exploit them - that was the 'way of the world' . Exposing these ideas is part of the job of sociology, showing how a 'critical awareness' of social life shows how it is constructed.

Watch Downton Abbey for a good example of false consciousness in every possible respect.

Comparing differences

Once we have seen that the way people behave isn't 'natural' or god-given, that common sense ideas are often false, then we can see how social behaviour isn't innate — it is all constructed or made up.

Comparing different societies shows the many different ways that people might behave, and that ultimately one way isn't naturally more sensible than any other.

Once you start to think about where you start with social behaviour, it soon becomes clear that the way people behave is mostly influenced by already existing patterns and modes of behaviour.

We learn our social behaviour in the family. The phrase 'bringing up children' actually means teaching them how to behave like proper social beings.

This is the key idea of 'Socialization'.

How to approach the study of sociology

So if we are going to begin studying sociology, where do we start?

So how do you study society?

It is often said that sociology is the scientific study of society and of human behaviour, but it is not immediately clear what that means.

You can't study society. You can only study people and how they interact.

Ah I know what you mean. Society is just an abstraction, you can't see it.

Society is structure and power. You can see it in action. The police are a symbol of society's laws and methods of control.

If you wonder why most judges in Britain are middle-aged white men who went to a few select public (private) schools you are asking a sociological question

Put in sociological terms the question would be "What sort of social structures are in place that leads to certain kinds of people getting certain kinds of jobs?"

A social structure is a stable pattern of inherited behaviour, or way of doing things, that persist in a given society. In particular the law is a set of rules that is drawn up and enforced by society. Who enforces the law is a different question, and how people come to be at the top of the social structure is something that sociology is interested in.

Class is very important social structure which has been much discussed, and in Britain we have a Royal Family, which sits at the very top of the social structure.

Being Royal is inherited, as is being upper class, so we have to ask what kind of equality do we actually have in Britain today.

How sociology would judge Judges

So, the legal system is a particularly strong social structure governing how everybody is supposed to behave.

There's one law for the rich and another for the poor!

The legal system is an institutionalised form of behaviour with deep historical roots. The courts, the police, jails and prisoners are all parts of the structure that everyone is used to, and mostly accepts as necessary and normal.

The whole of society is made up of clusters of these structures that all operate together (or in dispute) to make things work.

Examining how they work is somewhat more complicated though. When we look at the clash between the law and a member of an ethnic minority who has been routinely stopped by the police for no good reason we have to examine issues of culture, the definition of ethnicity, of ideology and of social control.

(The cases of abuse of young girls in Rotherham, by Asian men operating in gangs points out just how complicated these questions are.)

Does the 'Establishment' exist is another good question ?

The origins of sociology

Some of the ideas that sociologists discuss have always been talked about by philosophers, poets, novelists and even religious leaders. 2,500 years ago, in his book 'The Republic', Plato discussed how society should be organised.

But we don't call him a sociologist

القرآن الكريم

The Koran talks about how society should be organised and Confucius discussed the same thing in China 3,500 years ago.

Sociology just tries to make it more precise, more scientific and more coherent.

The beginnings of modern sociology lie in the science and philosophy of the "Great Enlightenment" in the 18th century.
At the root of these changes was a rational science, in opposition to religious belief and explanation.

Modernity

To put it rather crudely we can say that sociology is a reflection of the increased complexity of 'modern' society. By this we mean that only when society had been transformed into a recognisably 'modern' or 'industrial' society was it possible to begin to reflect on how that transformation had occurred.

To put this another way, social change in feudal and agricultural societies was often so slow that hardly anyone noticed it. Industrial society (capitalism) speeded things up so much it began to be obvious that society was in a state of flux, and needed to be regulated and controlled in very different ways.

Modernity and industrialization undermined the old settled order of agriculture and religion and began to speed up all of the technological and cultural changes that had developed over several centuries.

We can say that modernization (and this tricky new bit, 'postmodernity') is simply that process of change constantly speeding up.

When you grow olives in the same way for 2,000 years you think about the olives and not about change. This is probably why sociology wasn't invented by cavemen (or women) because they didn't have the intellectual tools to do it.

Sociology could only arise when the conditions of history allowed new forms of thinking to be given birth—sociology is modern.

It was during the intellectual revolution we call the 'Enlightenment' that change, progress and critical thought all combined to lead people to the realization that society, like everything else, was 'man-made' and therefore changeable.

In criticising the old order, a new vision of society was born, and the French revolution gave the stamp of approval to these radical new approaches. The French Revolution transformed society from top to bottom, got rid of the aristocracy and tried to introduce a classless society. (Good try but didn't completely work.)

Who founded Sociology?

Because the French Revolution (and later the American) led to an explicit idea of changing society embracing freedom and equality for all, thinkers got very interested in the idea of how society worked.

So who are the founders?

Comte, Durkheim, Monstequieu and the French Revolution.

Throwing out monarchies and rejecting religion raised many questions about who had the right to govern and how society should be organised. This, combined with the new scientific method of observation and the formulation of theories based on experimental data, contributed to the climate in which sociology emerged.

Basically, the French philosophers and thinkers who radically criticised the old society gave birth to both the Revolution and to what became sociology. This is not surprising because the French Revolution utterly transformed their society, invented the idea of democracy and freedom for all and kicked off what we now call 'modernity'.

We can trace the origins of sociology back, amongst others, to Baron Montesquieu's work 'The Spirit of the Laws' (1748) i which he considered the 'nature and principles' that underlay different kinds of laws, and therefore societies.

My radical proposal was to consider the different institutions in society and how they influenced each other or interacted.

The understanding that legal systems can be very different suggests that again such things are not set in stone but are made by man, and are therefore social. From this idea, it wasn't a great intellectual distance to think about society as a whole.

Most thinking about social forms had just concentrated on specific areas, like the economic or the religious. To begin thinking 'encyclopaedically' was in itself revolutionary.

As everybody knows, it was really the Scottish Enlightenment that started it all !

It is a grand theory that tries to explain, everythign about human development through analysis, comparison and theoretical evaluation of social institutions.

Where do we start ?

It is a male-dominated profession that seeks to explain social development in terms of male categories, like work, wealth, war and industry. It is completely blind to women and thier work, and their social roles.

What is Positivism?

Well, it is the science that the French philosopher **Auguste Comte** (1788-1857) Comte claimed to have invented. **(Course of Positive Philosophie)**

The sociological "positivism" I developed can be seen as a deeply conservative reaction to revolutionary politics. It was also the beginnings of the idea that rational social planning would solve all problems.

Positivism claimed to build scientific theories of society through observation and experimentation, thereby demonstrating the laws of social development. Comte argued that general laws could be produced from comparing the evidence that social observers could directly develop themselves. It was therefore empirical social observation.

Positivists believe in the unity of the scientific method.

We can objectively show how social structures work through quantifiable results.

Do you really think that human motivation can be studied like physics or chemistry?

This is a huge claim.

So you think social planning will produce social utopia, do you?

The Organic Model

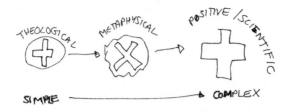

Comte's description of the development of societies said that they went from a theological stage, through a metaphysical stage to a positive or scientific stage.

This evolutionary outlook assumes that societies, like organisms, develop from the simple to the complex.

This organic analogy sounds quite plausible, but is now generally considered to be just another 19th century fantasy.

Comte was right about one thing though - that sociology is the most general and the most difficult of the human sciences.

Comte, and Spencer after him, believed that one had to look at 'consensus' in society, or the way in which total integration of the system as a whole worked.

Understanding the causal relations between social phenomena will unlock the future.

Indeed, every true science has for its object the determination of certain phenomena by means of others, in accordance with the relations which exist between them. Auguste Comte

Science will conquer everything.

It just tells us how dead white males like to make rules and feel that they control everything.

It's so simple isn't it?

Comte actually used the term 'sociology ' for the first time in the fourth volume of his giant work **Cours de Philosophphie Positive** (1838) . He was certain that sociology was a new science and that he would be recognised as its founding father – and he was right on both counts, just about.

The argument as to whether sociology is a science or not still rages, and most people think it isn't a pure science, but it does try and use scientific methods to understand the society that it observes. (The fact that society is made up of people is probably why it can't be a true science.)

A preview of feminist criticism

Anticipating the much later feminist criticism of sociology's masculine bias and approach, **Harriet Martineau** (1802-76) published a work that raised key questions about how women were marginalised in the theory. It had little impact at the time but became recognised as an important and interesting comparative analysis of social structure.

Her work raised the difficult question of how you understand societies that function in very different ways, and also the question of understanding the different role of women in society.

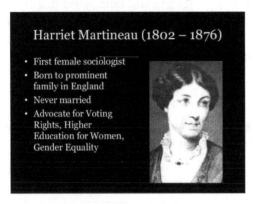

Harriet Martineau (1802 – 1876)

- First female sociologist
- Born to prominent family in England
- Never married
- Advocate for Voting Rights, Higher Education for Women, Gender Equality

'How to observe Manners and Morals' 1838, much more modest than Comte's great schemes, nevertheless put forward a methodology for sociological research which is just as important.

Her work was an early instance of what we might now call cultural studies, which is an important area of contemporary sociology.

Evolutionary Sociology

Following on from Comte, the next big name in the sociological hall of fame was Herbert Spencer (1820- 1903). His take on evolutionary sociology was very popular for a while but it also went out of fashion quite quickly in the development of sociology. With the impact of Darwin's theory evolution became a very trendy topic, which Spencer exploited, but the idea of social evolution as a natural process to explain social development didn't have much depth.

The Study of Sociology

Herbert Spencer

My approach was known as Social Darwinism , and implied that certain societies, especially Western ones, were superior and natural. The logic of this argument was that through natural selection, as in the world of animal species, societies evolved to higher levels.

If you believed this you might also think that there was no point in trying to influence the actual course of social development. (as it was a natural process it was inevitable and thus necessary?)

Spencer's **The Study of Sociology**(1873) was very popular at the time, especially with the ruling classes who could use it as an argument against the need for any social reform. Spencer is pretty well discredited today, although his form of Social Darwinism lives on in popular writing and neo-liberalism.

The idea that society is 'natural' and operates like an organism is a terribly strong common-sense idea that is sometimes called socio-biology – and means that people see the way society develops as natural and not to be criticised (which is a very reactionary view) 'the way things are meant to be'. Spencer, like Comte, was impressed with the natural sciences and wanted to make sociology a science.

So biological metaphors about society seemed to go hand in hand with proper scientific procedures.

What starts out as a respect for science, which seems fine, ends in the theoretical and political disasters of eugenics, racism, and, ultimately, the holocaust.

You were popular because you claimed that injustice and poverty were 'natural' and that social welfare was a waste of time.

Exactly, and my ideas keep coming back, like Thatcherism and Reaganism, and books like The Bell-Curve and all those debates about how some races have a lower IQ than others.

Spencer

History

Trendy

Shallow

You argued that society should be seen as a system, which is right, but the rest is Victorian social Imperialism, and proof of how pseudo-science can be a powerful ideology in social formations.

Spencer's grand theories have had little lasting influence in sociology, except perhaps in the theories of functionalism – which basically seeks to examine the social 'function' of an institution in society. It is thought that an institution (like prisons) survive because they fulfil an important social function – locking up criminals.

Sociology's search for general laws of society, and its sense of itself as a unified and all-encompassing science, are what makes it unpopular with historians, economists, philosophers, psychologists and politicians - whilst they tend to look at very small, specific areas of human activity, sociologists want to look at how the whole thing works, which is seen as over-ambitious.

Comte perhaps had a god-syndrome where he thought of himself as creating a new religion – which in itself is an interesting sociological phenomenon. (Think of Scientology)

It is odd that despite claiming to be scientific, sociologists have rarely spelt out the kinds of laws and generalizations they claim to be using.

The Generalizations of Sociology

Overall the kinds of very broad generalisations made in sociology can be summarised as:

1) That society can be studied in the same way as other scientific approaches, like chemistry.

2) That general laws about how society functions can be expressed (like Adam Smith's arguments about rational economic behaviour.)

3) That empirical correlations can be demonstrated between different social phenomena, like suicide and unemployment. (or religion and suicide.)

4) The tendency to make generalisations about the conditions under which institutions and societies arise (like the rise of capitalism.)

5) The tendency to make correlations between changes in one institution and another — between, say, changes in the organisation of religion and the economic mode of production.

6) A tendency to make generalisations about the evolution of human society (like Comte's theories of the three stages of development)

7) The claim that society can be understood as a general organism that functions in rational ways.

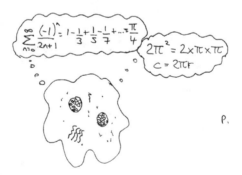

In the end none of these kinds of generalisations actually add up to universal laws which are verifiable, scientific or empirically proven.

Sociology makes these large claims but still has to try and substantiate them.

The contribution of Durkheim

The man who tried to rescue sociology and to establish scientific laws, to show that studying sociology was a proper academic discipline, was **Emile Durkheim** (1859- 1917). He basically followed Comte's line about creating a science of society and attempted to establish more precise, organised ways of defining the subject.

He became the first Professor of Sociology at the University of Paris - in fact the first anywhere - and his big themes examined 'consensus'- what held society together - and ways of seeing society as a complete system.

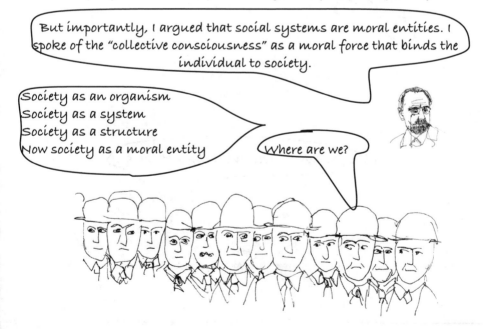

But importantly, I argued that social systems are moral entities. I spoke of the "collective consciousness" as a moral force that binds the individual to society.

Society as an organism
Society as a system
Society as a structure
Now society as a moral entity

Where are we?

Durkheim on Suicide

Durkheim's methods, in trying to develop scientific laws of sociology, can best be seen in his famous work on suicide.

Suicide seems like a very individual act, almost the most individual act, but Durkheim wanted to think about how the relationship between social structures and the individual might influence the actual event.

I decided to take this seemingly very individual act of ending one's life to see is there were any social patterns or forces at work. What are the moral pressures at work on the individual?
Could I just ask you a few questions? A little survey...it won't take long.

Durkheim

We positivists need our daily statistics.

In his famous work, simply called **Suicide**(1897), Durkheim looked beyond the individual act to think about the social factors that underpinned it. By comparing statistics from different societies Durkheim showed that there were in fact regularities in the patterns of suicide that demanded attention.

It was a very precise way of posing the key question of sociology - how does society influence the individual.

Notably, Catholic societies had a lower suicide rate than Protestant - the explanation being the strength of community and the anti-individualism of Catholicism.

Durkheim was here seeking to draw out the empirical correlations he had established between social integration and the suicide rate. Whether he did so or not is still debated. Some argue that what Durkheim demonstrated was that certain societies represent things in different ways

Durkheim described four types of suicide:

1) Egotistic
2) Anomic
3) Altruistic
4) Fatalistic

Father I feel like killing myself. I've done terrible things.

I thought there was only one kind, where you killed yourself, dead.

Well you'd better become a Protestant, because we don't allow suicide. For them, it's a matter of individual conscience. For us, it's the worst sin imaginable.

That is the empirical truth, but behind that there are strong collective forces operating on people, coercing them to do things.

What if I pretended to fall under a statue of the Virgin Mary? Would that be a sin or a statistical freak?

You'd have a long time in purgatory to work it out. Is purgatory a social fact, or where sociologists go to wait for results?

Fatalistic suicide, for example, we find in groups where there is excessive control, as in slave society (or North Korea).

46

Durkheim Quiz

Altruistic Suicide

What on earth is altruistic suicide?
This takes place in a society where the social bonds are very strong, what I call "mechanical solidarity" . This is suicide done for the sake of the group, rather like the Japanese rital suicide, seppuku, when things have gone wrong and the individual takes the blame.

Anomic Suicide

What about this rather strange sounding "anomic" suicide?
It relates to what I call "anomie", or a state of not knowing where you fit in. Like being homeless or being an orphan. You feel you don't belong. It means being in a state of "normlessness"- without the norms and rules that guide you in everyday life.
Ah, so this is a pretty modern thing , when people don't know where they fit in a complex, digital world.

And 'egoistical' suicide – what's that?
It's obviously just what it sounds like – individuals who take their own salvation seriously, it's a form of narcicism.

Social facts

Durkheim was very keen to show the workings of what he called 'social facts' – this was a key part of his approach to sociology.

For Durkheim 'social facts' were 'ways of acting, thinking and feeling, external to the individual, and endowed with a power of coercion, by which they control him.'

Religion is a pretty good example of a social fact, in the sense that religious ideas impact greatly on the way that individuals brought up in a particular religion behave (something that is very relevant today)

This means that certain structures in society are so powerful that they control the actions of individuals and can be studied objectively , as in the natural sciences.
This was positivism at its most extreme, thinking of social structures as being facts.

Durkheim

Durkheim

You positivists never get past the observable facts to understanding or explanation – analysis is more important than bare facts.

You leave out entirely what the individual thinks.

Society has a force of its own – individualism is a kind of illusion.

But you can't deny that I demonstrated a direct correlation between forms of society and suicide rates.

Mechanical and organic solidarity

Durkheim was trying to think about how society worked in the widest collective sense, that is the way in which communal action was necessary to make things work. So the key question is what holds society together, when it could so easily fall apart, as it often does in times of war.

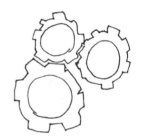

Durkheim used the idea of 'solidarity' to describe the glue that holds things together, and had a clear theory of the forms of this solidarity. He distinguished between two forms – mechanical solidarity – in more basic societies and organic solidarity- which develops in more advanced, complex societies.

To put it another way we can say that mechanical solidarity happens when the beliefs and outlook of a society are commonly agreed- often through religion- and social structures are fairly simple and stable. Like in Catholic Spain in the 15th century. This sort of 'collective conscience' holds everybody in place within a society and leads to basic agreement about how things should be run.

Organic solidarity on the other hand is what operates in more advanced, complicated industrial societies where social cohesion is going to be more of a problem, because everybody does not agree about the way things should be run. This is increasingly obvious in contemporary society.

In primitive societies, there is a form of "mechanical solidarity" at work. Society functions as a relatively close knit affair. Its culture and religion hold it together.

As society becomes more complex, through the division of labour , mechanical solidarity breaks down and is replaced by organic solidarity, that is more complexly constructed.

LESS COHESION

MECHANICAL
Organic

Durkheim argues that basically societies move from the simple form
of mechanical solidarity to the more complex form of organic solidarity
through the division of labour. (The way that people and jobs and skills are
organised)

As people move into the cities, which happens with industrialisation, the
competition for jobs and resources began to grow. Some people have
to become more specialised and some people lose out, and the pace of
change speeds up.

Specialised people

So the way that the division of labour is organised means that the
inter-dependence of people in society also changes – so the forms of
connection are not simple but organic, more based on necessity than on
belief.
The collective conscience, the cultural and religious beliefs, becomes
weaker but the necessary solidarity becomes stronger.

Structural sociology

As an established 'founding father' of sociology, it was right and proper that Durkheim should found a sociology journal (**L'Annee Sociologique**) and write a very great deal on many subjects. His first book was **The Division of Labour in Society** (1893) which deals with the moral basis of changes in the division of labour.

Then right through to his **Elementary Forms of the Religious Life (1912)** Durkheim always concerned himself with the collective function of any social activity, the way that individual acts always have a social dimension. These are what Durkheim calls social facts, the patterns of social organisation that express the moral order of society.

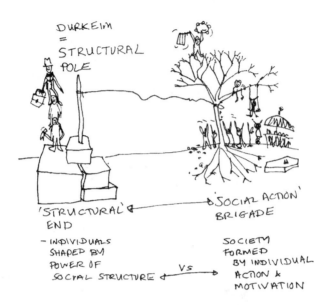

DURKEIM
=
STRUCTURAL
POLE

'STRUCTURAL'
END

→ 'SOCIAL ACTION'
BRIGADE

− INDIVIDUALS
SHAPED BY
POWER OF
SOCIAL STRUCTURE

Vs

SOCIETY
FORMED
BY INDIVIDUAL
ACTION &
MOTIVATION

Durkheim represents the structural pole of the debate in sociology between the 'structural' end and the 'social action' brigade, a debate that runs throughout sociology. On the one side people argue that it is only from individual action and motivation that society is formed (the social action lot) and on the other side are the structuralists who argue that individuals are shaped by the power of social structures.

This debate can also be represented as the ' consensus' versus the 'conflict' debate, in which society is either seen as an integrated whole composed of structures which fit together in a comprehensible way, or as patterns of conflict such as the battle between 'classes'.

CONSENSUS vs CONFLICT

CON SENSUS
    FLICT

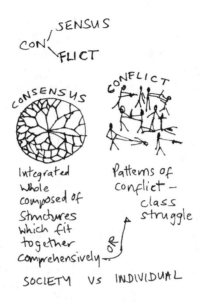

CONSENSUS

CONFLICT

Integrated
Whole
composed of
Structures
which fit
together
Comprehensively

Patterns of
conflict –
    class
    struggle

or

SOCIETY   vs   INDIVIDUAL

This is, kind of, society versus the individual, projected into a bigger pattern.

Individuals or groups are seen as battling to define society in their own interest, which means that society is not necessarily stable or integrated.

Marx's view of class conflict sees society as basically made up of opposing forces which constantly struggle against one another until strikes, revolutions or wars break out.

Marxian Sociology

The 'conflict' approach to sociology was developed in the 19th century by the quite well known Karl Marx (1818-93) He wrote a very great deal about economics, capitalism, culture, technology, class struggle and ideology. He also greatly extended that part of sociology which was concerned with grand theory, the evolution of humanity and the possibility of reconstructing society in an entirely different mode.

This was the sociology of class conflict, and of the laws of historical development.

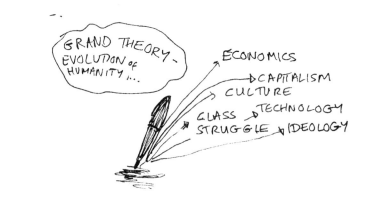

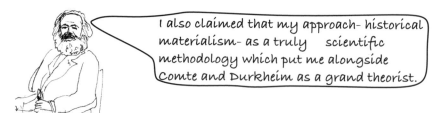

I also claimed that my approach- historical materialism- as a truly scientific methodology which put me alongside Comte and Durkheim as a grand theorist.

We can accuse Marx of ultimately producing the most totalitarian societies of the 20th century, despite setting out the most radical rhetoric of all time. This contradiction runs through all Marxist theory. Mind you, he was mega-correct about how technology would change the world.

Karl was mostly interested in social development and social change, and strongly believed that wealth and power were unequally distributed in society (pretty obvious really). He was therefore not interested in how social consensus functioned but in how one group in society maintained its dominance over another. (Class and rank)

CLASS
+
RANK

In some ways he had a functionalist approach in that he saw certain institutions in society working to maintain social cohesion.

Social Conflict

We can briefly sum up Marx's sociological approach as:

1) All societies are founded in conflict.
2) The basic motor of all social change is economic.
3) Society should be thought of as a totality in which the economic is the determining factor of all change.
4) Historical change and development is not random, but can be seen to relate to man's relationship to economic forms of organisation.
5) The individual is shaped by society, but can also change society through rational action based on scientific, historical materialist and revolutionary ideas.
6) That work in capitalist society leads to alienation and dissatisfaction.
7) By standing outside society, and through critique, human beings can understand and alter their historical condition.
8) Therefore through scientific critique and revolutionary action, society can be rebuilt.

This idea of social change proved to be a powerful idea in the 20th century. Now, in the 21st century it is now seen as an antiquated notion.

Kim Jong-un

Capitalism- a world wide system

Marx's central proposition was that capitalism was a new form of social organization based on exploitation of the workers by the owners of capital (the bourgeoisie). The capitalist class extracted surplus value from the worker, the proletarian class, and aggressively expanded and developed the technologies of production, thus creating a world-wide system. This is a very different picture of society from that argued for by Durkheim or Comte.

Present day globilized society shows exactly what Marx was talking about — the world economy is completely inter-connected.

My central argument is that the ways in which humans organise their economic production determines the overall shape of the society. Otherwise known as economic determinism. (i.e. the economic determines everything else.)

What Marx meant was that the forms of economic organisation - capitalist production for example - determine the law, politics, culture religion and ideology of society. This is known as economic determinism, or Marxism. It is a sociological claim of a strong universal law, of determinism, that many other sociologists disagree with.

What is the profit motive?

Money talks

Goal! come on you Reds!

Marx's sociology of capitalism argued that the profit-making production of commodities led inexorably to a certain kind of social system. This capitalist system is a reflection of this pursuit of profit. This idea is the very core of Marxian sociology.

The argument is that the values of capitalist production penetrate all spheres of society and set the agenda for the way that things are done, initially in business alone but ultimately in all aspects of society.

For example retirement homes for old people are now big business, and making money determines how many staff and what level of care is on offer.
This general idea represents what Marx meant by the economic infrastructure determining the superstructure – politics, culture, law, ideology etc.

Think about football over the last twenty years it has become a massive global industry, where money talks.

Now that the water we drink is owned by capitalist enterprises who make huge profits from selling water (which generally falls out of the sky) you can see what Marx was getting at.

Class Relations

Marx brought into sociology the very important idea of class, as opposed to groups, elites, people or castes. Marx argued that the membership of a social class was determined by the division of labour in a society.

Capitalism instituted a particular - and Marx argued a particularly exploitative - set of class relations. He argued that class was:

1) An objective, external structure.
2) Determined by the relationship to the means of production.
3) A key factor in the development of history.

All owners of capital share the same relationship to non-owners – that of exploitation (like zero hours contracts)

Class is a category that can exist but not be perceived by the mebers of that class. Bourgeois ideology obscures the reality (like the fantasy of the American dream – anyone can make it)

A Theory of Totality

For Marx, capitalist society inevitably produces class antagonisms (class war) rather than consensus and that was key to understanding society. Therefore because of the very structure of that society, conflict and disharmony were inevitable.

Marx synthesized everything that economists, political theorists and philosophers had to say about society to produce a grand sociological theory of capitalist society as a totality.

His arguments pervade much of sociology because he touched, directly or indirectly, of every area of thought within the sphere of sociology.

Marxist ideas of ideology, knowledge, culture and power still provide much of the framework within which sociological debates go on.

The ghost of Marx haunts all sociology.

Spectre
of
Marx

Weber's Sociology

Max Weber (1884- 1920)

Max Weber is the next big hitter in the Sociology team and, like Marx, he was concerned with the problem of stratification in society (class, elites, dominant groups etc). Weber took issue with Marx's views in society and class struggle and this became a major debate within sociology.

> I argued that it was the rise of a particular religious outlook, namely Protestantism, that distinguished certain societies and led them to develop capitalism.

Unlike Marx he wasn't terribly politically active and didn't claim to have solved all of the problems of how society functioned. His first major work **The Protestent Ethic and the Spirit of Capitalism** (1906) distinctly parted company with Marx about the origins and development of capitalism.

The Protestant ethic has an affinity with capitalism, Weber argued (they fitted together). This is a key, and interesting, idea.

The Problem
of Stratification

Understanding Social Action

Weber redefined the general theoretical approaches of sociology and did specific work on class and stratification, also the law, religion, capitalism, power, as it is exercised in society, the city, music and cross-cultural studies. Unlike Marx, who probably never used the word sociology, Weber systematically set out a philosophy of the social sciences and attempted a complete definition of sociology. He was interested in the way people behaved, and in how behaviour influenced the wider society, as well as its social structure.

Social action lies at the heart of the sociological approach, and only by understanding the intentions, ideas, values and beliefs that motivate people can you really know anything.

Verstehen

Suppose a poor, badly educated and "alienated' chlld throws a brick through Weber's window. Weber asks him:

Is that a good reason for this action?

No, but Smiths the window glaziers pay me to go around breaking windows.

Ah ich verstehen I understand. You break windows and I understand things sociologically. It's my job..

Weber's concern with 'understanding' (the Verstehen concept) may seem straightforward but it leads to that sociological approach we now call the 'scoial action' approach – which is about how a culture and individuals inter-react.

Bureaucracy

The other very important area in sociology that Weber pioneered was the study of the way in which modern societies became bureaucratic or controlling (the state that watches people) - the Big Brother syndrome. This also related to Weber's other big concern with what he called rationalization.

Why was that important?

Just get a ticket, stand in line, fill out the application form giving three references and we'll consider your application to ask a question.

I'm not really that interested.

In that case, fill out the withdrawal form, stand in line and fill in the application form to be considered for withdrawal.

Rationalization

Capitalist societies become increasingly like an "iron cage" Rationalization is the process by which every little part of society is subjected to analysis, organization, professionalization and bureaucracy.

Just as Marx used to point out that the rationalized reorganisation of production led to alienation, so Weber was concerned at the way in which the state constantly intervened more and more in the life of its citizens. This is a key idea of how the state remorselessly expands to control more and more of society. Present day surveillance makes this point very clear. (Britain has the most cameras of any advanced country.)

The Spectres of Communism and Bureaucracy

Despite his attacks on Marx, Weber often sounds like Marx when he is talking about rationalization.

Weber sounds like a determinist when he discusses it.

This is odd because Weber claimed to be mainly interested in understanding social actor's motives, not socially determining structures.

Weber often seems to argue that culture is more determinant than the economic in shaping society. However the way Weber talks about it culture sometimes seems to include the economic as an important force in shaping society.

Germany in this period , 1870- 1918, was going through major changes and industrialization, and the rise of a large communist party.

If we are polite, we can say that he could see both sides of the argument — and perhaps an extra one as well.

Weber was also very concerned with political groups, the complexities of social status and the 'charisma' of leaders — an idea of uncanny prescience, given the later rise of Hitler.

My attitude to sociology as a discipline can be summed up like this:

1) It could not develop scientific laws (anti-positivism)

2) It could not predict or evaluate future social development.

3) It could only use collective concepts like 'class' if they could be discussed in terms of individual action.

4) It could not prove any evolutionary development in human societies (anti-organicism)

5) It should construct models or 'ideal types' that could be compared.

6) It should aim for objectivity by systematic empirical research (by being 'value-free')

7) It could not draw on the natural sciences because it was about 'consciousness' not 'structures'.

Marx and Weber differ fundamentally. Marx was convinced that there were 'iron laws' of historical and social development and therefore a 'science of society' — historical materialism. Weber disagreed with this on every point.

Sociology is a science concerning itself with the interpretive understanding of social action, and thereby with an explanation of its causes and consequences. So all sociology is about social action, about the ways and means in which people interrelate with different kinds of societies. Trying to understand the different ways in which people relate within society inevitably leads to a theory of trying to classify what kind of society is being talked about.

Tonnies: Social Classifications

Tonnies

Another important German sociologist was **Ferdinand Tonnies** (1855-1936) whose interest in the forms of and patterns of social ties and organizations resulted in classifications of particular societies. He classified societies as either Gemeinschaft (community) or Gesselschaft (association).

A Gemainschaft society is one in which social relations are close, personal and valued by their members. The family is the basis of social networks, with social conformity as the norm. This sort of community is typical of pre-industrial society. The Amish in America today are representative of this form of society. (Albeit in a nostalgia mode.)

A Gesselschaft society is instead one in which close family associations have disappeared and in which social relations tend to be impersonal and non-kinship based. Social ties arise from an elaborate division of labour in which the work-place is more important than the extended family, as in today's society.

Tonnies basic theme is the loss of community and the rise of impersonality. These themes have become very important in the study of life in the modern city.

Changes in Sociology

We might add 'post-industrial' society to Tonnies classification (because that is the kind of society we now live in) but understanding social relations in this kind of society is quite tricky. Analysing the kinds of social relations in a particular society is one way of classifying what sort of social system it is. Throughout the history of sociology theorists have tried to classify different societies into neat patterns and definitions. Comte began this with an argument that there was an historical development towards a perfectly rational society. Marx encouraged this tendency by saying that you defined a society by its 'mode of production' or the form of economic organisation. Durkheim then distinguished between 'mechanical' and 'organic' solidarity (or forms of social organisation) Weber than argued that you could classify different types of authority as 'traditional', 'charismatic' and 'bureaucratic' (Types of society.)

The question is, is it possible to classify a whole complex society by one set of characteristics?

In simple societies definitely; in later societies, probably.

Can you see the coming chaos - the mass emigration to America?

The frontier —

When sociology emigrated to the United States in the 20th century, it found new problems and new methods. 19th century European sociologists had been preoccupied by societies in which large, powerful social groups or classes predominated with entrenched interests and cultures. (Like aristocracies and monarchies) American society was fundamentally more fluid and socially open. This is why 20th century social development and theory has always tended to look towards the American model for inspiration, rightly or wrongly. European society had taken millennia to develop and social change had been very slow. American society seemed to have developed overnight and without all that much awareness of where it was going. 19th century theorists could never have imagined the whirlwind of development that America initiated, in which traditional society was replaced by a mythology of the 'frontier'. (An idea of society emerging from nowhere as it were!)

Native American culture took thousands of years to develop and little more than 100 years to destroy. That is the other side of modernization.

The spread of mass industrialization

Since Marx and Comte were writing at the beginnings of mass industrialization it is not entirely surprising that their sociological views quickly dated. Marx's belief in inevitable revolution did not stand the test of time. Weber was quite certain that there was no inevitable process of revolutionary change.

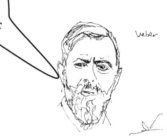

I can be seen as the sociologist who straddles the emergent societies of the 19th century and the increasingly complex and contradictory societies of the 20th.

The emergence of sociology in America

Sociology became popular in the United States largely because it was a society of high-speed change, development and experimentation.

It was also a pragmatic, capitalist society that worshipped production and economic expansion.

In one sense American society had to be invented because it had no history or back-story of organic development, but in another way it was firmly based in European models. (Going back to the Greeks) Perhaps because of its lack of roots, sociology in America concentrated on empirical study, trying to capture the factual details of what was really happening, rather than building grand theories of human development. Individualism and individual struggle were also greatly emphasized in American culture and philosophy.

It is a bit of a mystery, then, that functionalism, which so much assumes social order and cohesion, should have become the mainstream theoretical approach in America.

The Technological Revolution

The unleashing of technology, which Marx had correctly identified as the dynamic of development in capitalism, reached its fruition in the United States, and in so doing produced a new and radically different society . Henry Ford's production lines, and the new rationalized time-and-motion studies in the steel industries, were the beginnings of massive social change which was so radical that sociologists were always trying to catch up with it.

Technology transformed society and computing transformed technology, which than transformed society all over again.

It is not an exaggeration to say that virtually every aspect of modern capitalist society has been restructured and transformed almost every decade since the 1930's. In the last twenty years it has been revolutionized by the internet. The pace of change has also accelerated with every decade, now even three year old technology is out-dated.
Compare this with some agricultural technologies that have been used for 2,500 years in the Third World, and you get an idea of the difficulty of the sociologist's task.

Social change, social reform and social surveys are at the basis of all sociology, and all three were clearly evident in the industrializing and urbanizing America of the late 19th and early 20th centuries. One could also see the Protestant ethic at work in the cultural legacy of the early Puritan fathers of the East coast of the newly formed America. The ethic of hard-work, thrift, sobriety and avoiding the sins of the flesh were, as Weber had so interestingly argued, consistent with the new spirit of capitalism. 20th century America absorbed millions of migrants through a massive expansion of population, also had a strange history of slavery and exploitation which contributed to economic growth, and somehow made all of this work in an explosive development of production and technological change that transformed the world for everyone.

Sociology is a barometer of how people feel about society. It veers between orthodoxy and conservatism, with very occasional flashes of radicalism.

75

Pioneers of American Sociology

An odd character called **Lester F. Ward** (1841-1913) played an important role in the early history of American sociology. His whole working career was spent working for the United States Geological Survey.

I set out to identify the basic laws of social life, drawing on Spencer's approach, but I was also an advocate of social reform.

Addams

WEB. DuBois

Lester F Ward

Two other Americans of early major influence were **W.E.B. DuBois** (1868-1963) and **James Addams** (1860 -1935).

Both conducted detailed empirical surveys which clearly demonstrated what people's living conditions were actually like (An important aspect of sociology). The function of this investigative research - actually demonstrating what was happening in society - became an important part of American sociology.

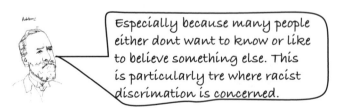

Addams

Especially because many people either dont want to know or like to believe something else. This is particularly tre where racist discrimation is concerned.

W.E.B. DuBois's study **The Philadelphia Negro** (1899) carefully depicted the actual living and working conditions of black people, and the reality of racism and discrimination.

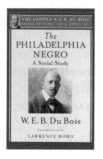

I was the first black sociologist to gain academic acceptance and was also active in the National Association for the Advancement of Coloured people. (NAACP).

Jane Addams' famous **Hull House Maps and Papers** (1895) were a detailed documentary of the slum conditions in Chicago's West side.

My survey gave impetus to social reform.

Jane Addams

This kind of empirical research that demonstrates what is actually happening in society becomes more important all the time. This is basically because as society gets ever more complex, which it certainly has done in the last decade, it seems that individuals know less and less about how other people actually live. (And the question of the digital age looms over everything to do with sociology)

The mass media seem to cover everything but it is debatable whether they increase or decrease knowledge about actual social conditions. The American insistence on empirical investigation was highly productive in many senses, but constantly ran up against commonsense ideas and entrenched ideological positions.

It was recognised that social reform was necessary however, and this gave added impetus to the growth of sociology as a discipline in the United States. Sociology is always directly affected by the political climate of the times, unlike biology or physics.

The Chicago School

The first department of sociology in America was founded at the University of Chicago in 1892. It was famous for two things: its urban studies – not surprising given its place in a large city- and its championing of symbolic interactionism, which is more surprising. The empirical study of the city meant that urban studies could take Chicago as a kind of 'laboratory'. This same kind of interest led to a concern with symbolic interactionism – which was all about trying to figure out how people interact in a face to face situation.

When you live in a crowded city you obviously have more inter-action than if you live in the middle of nowhere, and this changes cultural inter-action.

79

Urban sociologists

The Chicago sociologists did not look at society as a whole, or as a mega-system that controlled everything, but at smaller groups and how they made sense of their place in society. Because Chicago was a rapidly growing and multi-ethnic society, they could see before their own eyes a whole new social process. Immigrant cultures set up their own sub-groups in ghettos where standard white American ideas were out of place. The Chicago school produced a series of studies looking at groups and gangs seen as deviant or non-conforming.

To do this, we had to engage in direct study, and develop a new theoretical approach that took account of the way in which people defined their new situation.

KU Class of 1895. The arrow points at Stanton Olinger. He completed the first PhD in Sociology in 1916.

People develop and define their group identity through inter-action – a mutual working out of what things mean. This is the creation of the "social self".

Culture and Meanings

The meanings that people give to their cultural and social activities are as real in their consequences as economic forces and political changes. Wage rates may seem very real, but then so are people's ideas about what work is and what leisure is. Religion is the most extreme example of the power of ideas, for which people have died throughout history. Culture basically functions through groups, large and small.

Chicage school analysis is very concerned to look at how individual's perceptions of their situation shape their culture and group responses. The Mafia is the most extreme form of this kind of group culture.

Urban studies

Understanding how a city functions becomes increasingly important in 20th century sociology, as the world gets more urbanized. The Chicago School, and especially **Robert Park** (1864-1944) came to dominate urban studies. Park developed what he called the 'sociological approach' by which he meant that the city somehow adapted itself in an orderly fashion to development, rather like the way that ecological processes adapted to the changing nature of the world.

A city is, it seems, a great sorting and shifting mechanism, which, in ways that are not wholly understood, infallibly selects out of the population as a whole the individuals best suited to live in a particular region and a particular milieu.

Robert Park

Louis Wirth (1897- 1952), another Chicago school sociologist, viewed Urbanism as a "way of life" similar to Weber's idea of 'impersonal' city life. The idea, dominant in modern sociology, that the city stands for alienated, impersonal social relations, is something of a myth. Cities vary as much as the countryside and change as slowly or as rapidly as any other part of society. The basic assumption that all city life is fast, dangerous and unpleasant, whilst all country life is slow, charming and friendly, does not stand up to the most elementary empirical research. Inner city life can be friendly, cosmopolitan, interesting and socially interactive, as opposed to isolated, alienated and often hard country life.

The myth of the countryside has existed since the Romans complained about city life 2,000 years ago.

The question is not so much about the city as an abstract entity, but the meanings that people give to it.

Symbolic Interactionism

This approach to sociology, pioneered by the Chicago school, was precisely to do with the sorts of meanings that individuals give to their environment- how they define their view of the world.

This relates to the complicated questions of identity and socialization – or how people learn their culture and reproduce it. (Living the culture you are born into.)

While much of 19th century sociology concerned itself with the 'grand schemes of things' symbolic interactionism saw itself as bringing things down to the basics - that is, to individuals and how they make sense of the world.

This is the individualistic end of social theory, which sees society as constructed of the individual's acts and intentions. It fits with the American ideas of the free spirit and an open society.

The 'Social Self'

George Herbert Mead (1863- 1931) the man responsible for this approach, pointed out that man is the only species that can use language, and therefore plan, think and communicate about experience.

As we develop as individuals, we learn to use the symbols of our immediate group and to give them the same meaning.
As we and society develop, these symbols and their meanings can change. Thus we symbolically interact with our environment.
Childhood shapes the personality forever. The self is always in process. Mead came to look at society in a similar way to that of Freud and psychoanalysis, but with a behaviourist twist. How the personality developed was seen as the central building-block of all social theory. Mead patented a theory of the self as constructed and reconstructed through interactive behaviour.

Am I self-made?

Mr Mead, tell us about your theory

It's about understanding the development of the self, the person, and imagining yourself in other social roles.

By having a sort of internal conversation with yourself- about 'significant' other people and other roles, you develop an idea of how everything works. Children do it very easily because they like to play roles and pretend to be other people. This is practising for growing up.

Exactly. The development of the self is a process between the "I" and the "me". So it's about human agency- how I shape "Me" in relation to others.

Argument with Mead

All this stuff is fine, but it completely ignores the real pressures that society puts on people. You can't just choose to be a certain kind of person. All previous sociology showed how people are a product of their situation.

Your interactionist theory is only extrme individualism dressed up as group relations.

M: Not at all, you've missed the point.

M: The self can only develop in its interactions with other people, so that the self really is social - part of a group, a sub-culture, a wider culture. That's the point. Without other people to learn from , since the earliest days of childhood, there is no way for an individual to acquire a sense of self.

It's still all a bit voluntary though, isn't it? As though you can choose who you'll be today?

M: Not at all. Each socialized person is a society in miniature!

SOCIALISED PERSON

Symbolic Interactionism and Psychoanalysis

The Symbolic Interactionist approach, like psychoanalysis, is part of the attack on social system theory that happens every so often in sociological battles. The real difference is that psychoanalysis believes in the power of the unconscious to shape the individual, whereas the interactionists see it as a more conscious process. Both approaches give due importance to the problem of socialization, or how children are trained to become proper people and citizens. Both suggest that the clue to understanding society lies in the mind and the individuals' appropriation of external reality.

Psychoanalysis believes that childhood and the family define most of society's functioning. Symbolic interactionism says that the personality isn't fixed, but fluid. Psychoanalysis was pretty big in the States, but sociologists steered clear of all that sexuality stuff. They have a bad enough reputation as it is.

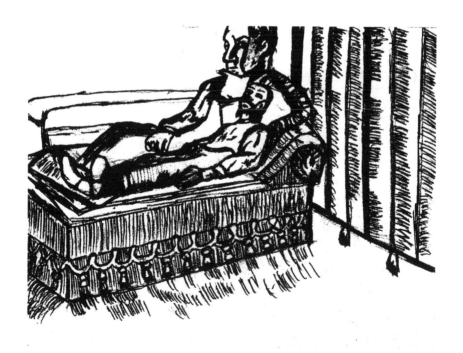

The Individual

There are two reasons for looking at socialization and how the personality is formed. First is the point that commonsense begins with the idea of the individual and second, that we have to understand the individual before we can properly understand the social. Funnily enough Pliny the Elder, the Roman encyclopaedist of the 1st century A. D., said the same thing.

Pliny: Man can neither speak, nor walk nor eat, and in short he can do nothing at the prompting of nature only, but weep.

Nature v Nurture

Do we just 'naturally' do things, like learn a language or behave in a certain way?

There is actually not very much evidence for this argument although people often believe it. On the other hand, for example, there are cases of children being brought up by animals and behaving like them.

These events demonstrate that becoming a civilized human being is learnt, though example, training and teaching. Human babies cannot do anything and therefore have to learn everything. (this is called socialization).

If learning is arrested in the early years, there is little chance of fully recovering from it. The process of learning is a very long one involving parents, schools, the mass media, friends, college and peer groups.

The nature supporters claim genetics and hormones make boys and girls. The nurture lobby says that it comes from social engineering.

How Does Socialization Function?

Socialization is a key concept in sociology. It connects one generation to another, and hugely reinforces the developing shape of society.

In fact, it is the only way in which society and culture can be reproduced. It is an area of constant moral panic over popular culture and other influences which supposedly shape a delinquent or deviant generation.

Trying to understand how individuals are shaped through socialization is a particularly tricky question, and that is where Freud's theories of child-formation become important.

Freud's Theory

That infant sexuality is at the basis of all human development is clear to me.

For Freud, the developing relationship of the infant to the mother, and father, profoundly affects the psychological make-up of the child. This process determines the later development of the individual through the power of the Unconscious, which is the repressed elements of this original relationship. The main sociological point here is that the creation of the personality, even in its hidden parts, is fundamentally social. Freud's idea is that the human personality is formed in a reciprocal relationship with the parents (which is a basically social process) In acquiring a sense of self, the infant picks up social ideas about gender, behaviour and cultural patterns. To be human means to develop a 'self' from social relationships with others.

Freud claimed to have discovered infant sexuality and the Oedipus Complex that goes with it. Not everybody agrees.

Much mainstream sociology dislikes Freud and psychoanalysis, claiming that it is unscientific and abstract. But in fact Freud was quite possibly right about the nature of the unconscious and its effects on the social - but if he was right this would undermine a lot of empirical sociology, which likes to discuss rational individuals.

Similarly, symbolic interactionism is not wildly popular because it undermines a lot of grand theories and sociological research projects. Actually Mead didn't use the term 'symbolic interactionism' – it was invented by one of his followers, **Herbert Blumer** (1900-87). Blumer put forward three propositions:

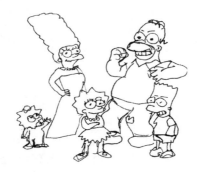

Human beings act towards things on the basis of the meanings that things have for them.

The meaning of things is derived from the social interaction that one has with one's fellows.

Group action takes the form of a fitting together of individual lines of action.

Functionalism

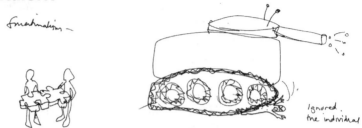

Ignored the individual

Sociological approaches seem to produce their opposites in historical terms, and symbolic-interactionism was counteracted by functionalism. This approach basically ignored the individual and concentrated on society as a system.

From the earliest days of sociology, the functionalist perspective has been important, perhaps because it approximates to a commonsense view of the world. This means that functionalists believe that all social institutions have a purpose within society —like the family - and that sociology is all about understanding that function. Functionalists in America, like Talcott Parsons and Robert Merton, are mainly interested in the large-scale structures of society - social classes, economic institutions , governments, armies etc, and the individual is seen as unimportant.

Talcott Parsons   Robert Merton

Functionalism became the dominant theoretical approach in America during the 1940's and 50's, but in the 1960's interactionism, ethnography and feminism began to undermine it.

94

Talcott Parsons

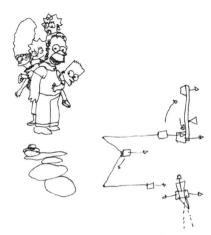

Talcott Parsons (1902-79) systematized earlier formulations of functionalist approaches to sociology, often in obscure, dry and pseudo-scientific fashion. He started from the 'Hobbesian problem of order' (what makes society orderly?) which goes back to the philosopher **Thomas Hobbes** (1588-1679).

Hobbes thought that people would naturally probably rip each other apart unless socially controlled and restrained. Parsons' major book **The Social System** (1951) set out at great length what he called the functional prerequisites of a society's survival. These were:

1) Adaptation- how a social system adapts to the environment.
2) Goal attainment- setting goals towards which a society's members are orientated.
3) Integration- the need to maintain social cohesion.
4) Pattern maintenance- socialization or reproducing society so that its values are maintained.

Equilibrium

In trying to answer the question about what causes social change, Parsons produced ingenious explanations to show how things could change but stay the same. This was his theory of equilibrium (balance). This theory suggests that changes in one part of the system produce counter-actions in other parts of the system which returns to equilibrium — even if it is a changed equilibrium.

think Parsons talks a load of old turnips, as we say round here.

If the democratic party system fell apart, then perhaps the military would step in to restore order, and then you'd have fascism, but also equilibrium. Or just a different kind of social order?

The case for a functionalist approach is that it does try to explain how society reproduces itself. New generations are born all the time that have to be socialized, educated, and taught how to become a part of society and how to find a role.

I harnessed Freud to discuss the problem of socialization.

Parsons said that social life is characterized by 'mutual advantage and peaceful cooperation', but he was probably quite wrong in his explanation.

Functionalism as an approach is the nearest thing that sociology ever had to a complete consensus, and Talcott Parsons was the King. During the golden years of the 1940's and 50's, almost everybody in America was a 'functionalist', possibly because almost everyone believed in the family, home-cooking and mother's place in the kitchen.

Clearly, a theory of a stable society and the belief that society is stable, homogenous and nearly perfect, go hand in hand. All parts of the system are interconnected and everything is integrated.

Somewhere there is a basic set of pressures which work towards the maintenence of stability. So if the family goes off the rails, then society will compensate by strengthening another part of the social structure. (The conservative basis of these arguments is pretty obvious!)

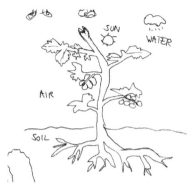

Functionalists like to make tidy arguments about everything and make lists of the functional prerequisites of society. These lists are the basic necessary conditions of existence which a society must meet if it is to survive, in the way that a plant needs air, water, and soil in order to live.

These supposedly 'universal' functional prerequisites of society are, of course, very like the 'hard' facts and general laws that one finds in physics and which 'hard' sociologists are always eager to invent and display. The problem is that society can be anything you want it to be - it doesn't really have a 'function'.

If you believe that society and all its members must be seen as a total system, then the functionalist approach becomes essential, and understanding conformity is a functional prerequisite of being a sociologist.

Unfortunately, the 1960's blew a hole in this normative utopia because hardly anyone conformed to it.

The idea that you can only study any part of the system in relation to the whole is actually what Marxists say, in a different way.

Main Functional Prerequisites

A rough list of some of the main functional prerequisites that one would look for in a society would be:

1) Social Control – How to keep things turning.

2) Socialization – To pass on the rules.

3) Adaption- The need to produce food and materials.

4) A belief system- Religion or ideology, so that a shared set of values and cultures is passed on.

5) Leadership- A person or group to make things happen.

6) Reproduction- A set of rules within which sexual activity and bringing up the young can happen.

7) Social Stratification – To ensure that the right sorts of people run things.

8) The Family- To ensure reproduction.

Merton's Functionalism

Robert K Merton (b. 1910) was a functionalist who tried to answer two fundamental questions in sociology. The way he did this oddly led to something of a crisis in the functionalist school of thought. The questions were:

1) Why should we view society as a whole?
2) Why should we assume a tendency towards conformity and integration?

In trying to answer these questions Merton put his finger on the basic fallacy of functionalism – the myth of coherence. (the idea that everything is organized and inter-related.)
There were three main problems in the functionalist approach which, in the wordy way of functionalists, Merton called " fallacious hypotheses" (being wrong!)

Fallacy 1: The postulate of indispensability (you can't leave it out) .
This begs the question of how any particular social institution actually reflects a " functional" or "essential' prerequisite of social order. (Why is it necessary?) This becomes a tautology, since in order to understand the function of something in society, you already assume it does have a function, which then explains why it is there. But if it weren't there, it wouldn't have a function.

Functionalists try to have their structure and eat it.
Or which comes first, the function or the function?

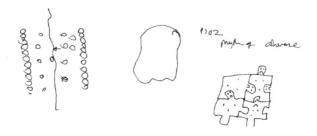

Fallacy 2: The Fallacy of functional Unity. (Why are things coherent?) In other words, why on earth should we assume that societies are integrated, coherent systems? Many societies are clearly nothing of the sort. How, for example, can functionalism explain societies that appear to be in constant conflict?

Would functionalists argue that the purpose of civil war was to produce harmony and integration?

> I tried to get around this one by making a distinction between the latent and manifest function of different kinds of behaviour.

> This means that people might appear to be doing something for one reason (the manifest) but its function for society might be something else (the latent).

Or, if the manifest explanation doesn't work, then talk about the 'latent' (or hidden) function, to get you off the tautology hook. War may have a manifest function of attacking the other side but its latent function might be to bring everyone together in the long term.

Fallacy 3: Sometimes called the 'the postulate of universal functionalism' or 'why does everything have to have a function?'

Who gives it a function? Does somebody collecting Barbie dolls have a function for the maintenance of society? Why isn't it just mindless, irrelevant stupidity with no function at all? Because Barbie dolls represent the best of American womanhood and function as an ideal for little girls. The function of Barbie dolls is to make money and give people anti-social ideas about what girls should look like.

What Merton says in response to the universal functionalism question is that one can distinguish between functions (or eufunctions) and dysfunctions. He argues that the functionalist approach isn't necessarily about how society actually works but is really just a method of analysis.

You can distinguish certain areas of behavior that could be dysfunctional in a society and yet somehow not be a problem for the overall analysis. (An odd bit of behavior doesn't invalidate the overall argument)

So how do you decide what is dysfunctional and what isn't? Claiming that deviance or criminality, for instance, actually has a function for society is weird. (How is crime good for society?) Yet this is exactly what Durkheim said about crime.

Does Inequality have a function?

This question about inequality in society is very topical, as inequality has grown in America and in Britain in the 21st century. Functionalists argued that inequality was found in all societies and was therefore necessary. Class, stratification, elites, whatever you want to call it, fulfilled a function which the functionalists described as making sure that the best people were in the top jobs. This bit of tautological nonsense (everyone in an elite group is brilliant?) greatly endeared functionalists to those who ran things.

Which brings us to the really serious charge against functionalism. Was it simply an acceptance and apology for the status quo?

Functionalism was unhistorical, uncritical and unable to examine the real complexities of people and society.

The real question that functionalism never answered is why societies change so much and apparently so randomly.

Conflict Theory

Functionalism, as a theory, had an inability to explain conflict, disharmony, power relations and class war — quite a list. This means that as a theoretical approach it had distinct limitations, as well as some strengths. Conflict theory was a reaction to the dominance of functionalist theory in the 50's and 60's and argued that, in fact, society was made up of conflicting groups who slugged it out most of the time. (rather than all hanging in together as one big happy family). The conflict theorists argued that the real focus of all social activity was conflict over land, resources, wealth, the means of production, water, housing, education, etc.

From this perspective, it is much easier to understand what makes society work. Institutions can be seen as mediating between social groups.

Social order is basically precarious and may break down.

But you don't have to be Hobbes or Machiavelli to think that people compete for scarce resources and wealth.

Marxian Conflict Theory

Karl Marx was one of the original and best known conflict theorists, most famously expounded in the **Manifesto of the Communist Party** (1848).

"The history of all hitherto existing society is the history of class struggles".

Most modern sociologists think this is going a bit far, but agree that conflict rather than consensus is the basis of society.

George Simmel (1858-1918) is also an important figure here.

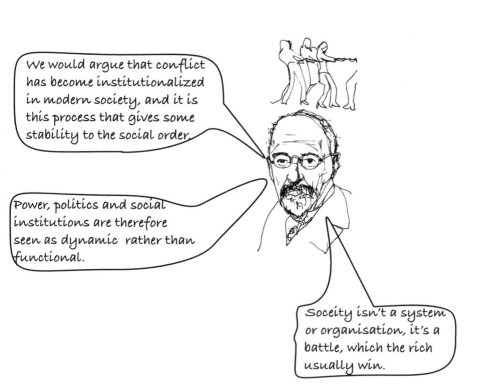

We would argue that conflict has become institutionalized in modern society, and it is this process that gives some stability to the social order.

Power, politics and social institutions are therefore seen as dynamic rather than functional.

Soceity isn't a system or organisation, it's a battle, which the rich usually win.

A Value Free Sociology?

Poincare

A French mathematician called Henri Poincare (1854- 1912) described sociology as the 'science with the most methods and the fewest results' (quite a good joke). This jibe upsets sociologists who like to claim that they always base their work on empirical evidence. In sociology it is always the 'other side' who engage in too much theoretical argument.

Sociology is meant to be synoptic (covering everything) but it hardly ever produces analyses that everyone (or anyone) agrees with. Sociology is like conflict theory in action. This is very odd, for what is meant to be a science. That's because sociology's object of study – society- changes faster than sociology itself. Sociology is inevitably forced to be a self-reflexive subject. It is also true that however much sociologists like to pretend otherwise, they are implicated in what goes on in society. Something can only be value-free if it is conducted in a cave 5,000 miles away, and even then there are shadows to contend with.

Towards Postmodernism

There is in fact a 'sociology of sociology' (or sociology of knowledge) which looks at the rise and fall of the ways in which different theoretical explanations of society develop, and how they try and discuss society. Since the decline of functionalism, which was closely linked to the conservatism of the post-war boom years, when everything seemed stable and fixed, sociology has fragmented somewhat into many different competing approaches. Since the internet arrived and transformed society again, all general theories of society have been thrown into disarray.

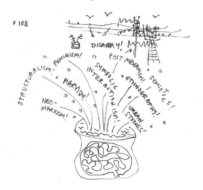

There is Marxism, symbolic interactionism, feminism, ethnography, urban studies, neo-Marxism, structuralism, semiotics and postmodernism, which have all fed into the post 1960's unraveling of a fixed discipline. As society changes ever more quickly, methods of thinking about how it works need to change as well, but often don't. Contemporary society is vastly different to the world of the pre-internet.

Jean Baudrillard says that we now live in a society which is completely hyperreal. This means that traditional society gets nowhere, because no one even knows what really goes on in society now, never mind understanding the function of it.

C. Wright Mills

An innovative thinker, C. Wright Mills provided a critique of both the status quo of sociology and of the self-complacent power elites in America, as well as an historical interpretation of the development of American sociology. His most famous work **The Sociological Imagination** (1959) savaged the complacency of functionalism and its cosy relationship with power elites in an attack that set the tone for the revival of critical sociology in the 1960's. Social inequalities and elites go hand in hand, and clearly a sociology that is deeply critical of wealth and power will inevitably not be popular with the power elites and the rich. C Wright Mills re-opened all of the questions that the conflict theorists had posed earlier.

This has been the conundrum of sociology since the 1960's — whether to be critical and thought provoking or to be quietly empirical and merely provide value-free information on what happens in society.

If sociology is doing its job properly, then it should annoy those in power, since it exposes what is actually happening.

Post 1960's Developments

Before sociology loses itself in the Baudrillardian simulacrum of post-modernity there are some salient points about the post-1960's developments of sociology that need to be considered. Among the most important are the return of Marxism, the rise of feminism, and the development of anti-colonialist theory of historical development.

Sociology had long talked about industrial society, capitalism and modernization, but it seemed to have forgotten that much of this was built on the back of an Imperialism that subjugated the Third World in order to pay for such development. The slave trade stands out as an historical thread that connected Britain and America to their colonies without ever impinging on the advanced social consciousness of scientific sociologists.

The other main point was that the sociological approaches derived from New Left Marxism were not connected to the politics of Communist countries, and produced critiques both of socialism and capitalism. Marxism, despite its flaws, is essential to sociology, because sociology is centrally about industrial society.

The End of Ideology

Perhaps the high point – or the low point, depending on how you look at it - of sociology as conformity was what came to be known as the 'end of ideology' debate of the 50's and 60's. This was when society was being seen as at its most advanced and therefore fixed for all time. **Daniel Bell** in his book **The End of Ideology** (1960) put forward the idea that class ideologies naturally declined in capitalist societies and that a convergence towards power-sharing and social harmony was inevitable.

Feminism, likewise, lobbed a large theoretical hand-grenade into the fantasies of functionalism, and blew up slightly more than a Parson's nose! Marxism obviously came as a total relief to this suburban fantasy of conformity.

FANTASIES OF FUNCTIONALISM...

Gramsci's concept of hegemony

I pointed out that the bourgeoisie did not rule by force alone but also by consent, forming political alliances with other groups and working ideologically to dominate society. In other words, society can be seen as unstable entity.

This important theorist redefined the way that Marxism thought about capitalist society. Marx had originally argued that capitalist society would become ever more polarized between workers and bourgeoisie. Since this fairly clearly did not happen in the West during the 20th century, but rather the opposite, Marxists had to rethink how capitalist society worked. It was increasingly recognized that society was becoming more, rather than less, complicated and that there were more classes and intermediate groups in society.

Antonio Gramsci (1891- 1937) was a key thinker in redefining the debate about class and power. His concept of hegemony has come to be central in sociological discussions of modern society.

Gramsci replaced Marx's notion of the inevitable class struggle in society with a more flexible view of the conflicts between groups, parties, individuals and ideologies. The idea of hegemony, or winning leadership, by consent in society, draws attention to the fact that individuals are always reacting to and redefining the society and culture they live in.

Ideologies aren't simply injected into passive subjects who live them out - they are areas of debate and battle between dominant and subordinate groups in society.

His ideas have had a lot of influence in cultural studies and in discussions about popular culture - which is no longer considered just 'circuses for the masses'. Looking at how culture actually works and how 'hegemonic' leadership functions in cultural battles made Gramsci an important contributor.

Gramsci wrote most of his theories in prison and so had to disguise what he was saying, because of the censor etc. This makes interpretation of his work just that bit more difficult.

Pessimism of the spirit; optimism of the will.

The Frankfurt School

This group of German critical theorists were mostly ignored when they wrote in the 1930's and 40's but began to be noticed in sociology in the 1960's. Again one of their central concerns was how culture worked in modern society, and their experience of Nazi Germany influenced their ideas, particularly on propaganda and mass culture. They were also concerned with the problem that society, although capitalist, did not seem to be displaying the simplistic revolutionary development that Marx had predicted.

There was class conflict but also cultural economic dommination that seemed to be taking on new forms.

We married Freud and Marx to come up with a new theory.

The failure of Marxism, both as theory and in practice in Russia, led us to develop a radical, critical theory of both

Marxism's failure to conceptualise the individual in society, the subject in sociology, was an important starting point for us.

Max Horkheimer

Theodor Adorno

irgen bermas

The Frankfurt school therefore set out a theoretical programe that included:

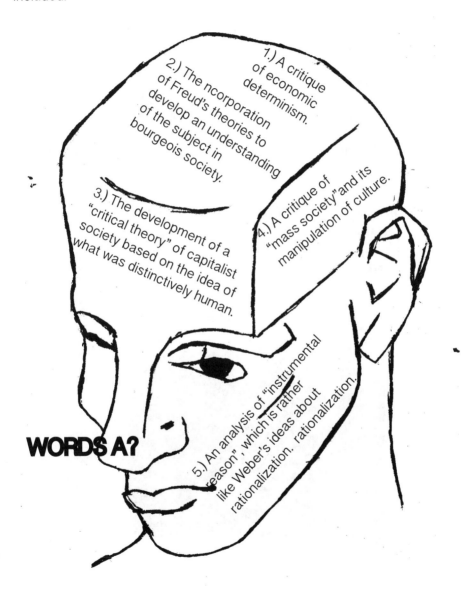

1.) A critique of economic determinism.

2.) The ncorporation of Freud's theories to develop an understanding of the subject in bourgeois society.

3.) The development of a "critical theory" of a capitalist society based on the idea of what was distinctively human.

4.) A critique of "mass society" and its manipulation of culture.

5.) An analysis of "instrumental reason", which is rather like Weber's ideas about rationalization. rationalization. rationalization.

WORDS A?

The Frankfurt school were also rather philosophical, and emphasized the importance of culture and ideology in shaping the individual in mass society, but many felt that they were too pessimistic in their gloomy view that mass culture was blinding everyone to the realities of life. The rise of Fascism and of what they called the "culture industries" seemed to them like similar signs of a new type of society that controlled its members through sophisticated cultural manipulation.

Their central argument about modern culture and the mass media is clearly an important one in modern sociology, but perhaps Gramsci's ideas about contested cultures are more appropriate in terms of modern sociological theory. They saw the 'culture industries' as completely manipulative, dominating society, but in the age of the internet almost anything is possible.

We argued that only "high culture" still retained a critical view of society, a sort of ivory tower against the debasement of the new media culture.

Herbert Marcuse (1896- 1979) a semi-detached member of the Frankfurt School, became very famous during the 1960's for his support of radical and anti-authoritarian causes. He was once called the 'grandfather of terrorism' , a reference to his critique of capitalist society **One Dimensional Man** (1964) which clearly brought together the Frankfurt School arguments that capitalism generated false needs, false consciousness and a mass culture that enslaved the working-classes. This became a big hit in the radical 1960's culture and he almost became a pop-star.

Unlike the others in the Frankfurt school, however, I argued for an authentic opposition and for liberation.

His other big hit, **Eros and Civilization** (1955) , is an important work in the debate about sexuality and society, and in 'Negations' (1968) he attacked sociology's pretensions to understand society. He is really a bridge between the old theoretical concepts of European sociology and the re-worked radicalism of the 1960's.

Jurgen Habermas

Post 1960's sociology increasingly became aware of culture and communication as significant factors in analyzing society. Jurgen Habermas (b 1929) combined these concerns with those of the Frankfurt School. His big theme was rational communication and of the possibility of it existing in modern capitalist society. Unlike the older Frankfurt School members he was not completely pessimistic about such a possibility and in his **The Theory of Communicative Action** (1981) he put forward a complex analysis of contemporary capitalist society. He was examining the effects of instrumental reason on society (What Weber had called rationality) and how this can be resisted through moral and communicative emancipation. Instrumental reason can be seen as the pragmatic logic by which capitalist society organizes everything in terms of better production (like mass assembly)

- and then he is interested in how through communication, man can resist this logic.

He is difficult, demanding and comprehensive, and tries to marry the determinist strands of the Frankfurt school and the action-based ideas of its American opponents.

The Structuralist Approach

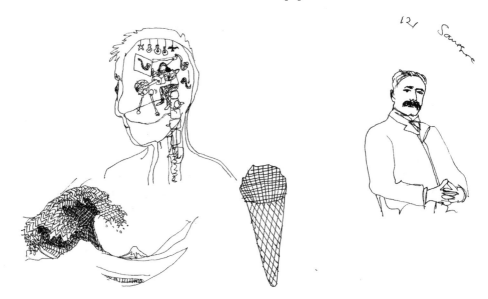

After the neo-Marxist shift in sociology came the wave of structuralist theory, which once again rewrote the ways in which social determination and social agency were thought about. The pioneering work in linguistics of **Ferdinand de Saussure** (1857-1913) began as a study of language but ended in studying almost everything as structure, including society. Saussure's theory of semiotics, or the study of signs, filtered into sociology in the post-1960's shift into more pluralistic theoretical approaches.

Seen as highly theoretical and "continental" , these structuralist approaches have been popular with some sociologists.

Particularly through the work of **Roland Barthes** (1915-80) and **Claude Levi-Strauss** (1908- 2009), structuralism has had a strong impact on many areas of sociology.

Starting from the famous axiom that language is a structured system, culture was then examined as a similar structured system, and then eventually society as a whole. Everything was considered as a structure, and the question of the relations of the parts to the system became paramount.

The most relevant part of the structuralist enterprise for sociology is in the area of cultural studies, or as sociologists say, in the analysis of culture as a signifying system. If this sounds a bit baffling it is because this was a radical new way of looking at things, one that 'de-familiarizes' the ordinary social world of common-sense. Instead semiotics look at how things 'signify' or come to have a meaning within culture.

A word "dog" signifies dogginess because our language system, through its rules and conventions, arbitrarily says it does. Everything, like a "flower", has a meaning because of the language system within which we operate. And since we are all caught up in this language system, how we understand things is also determined by that system.

The argument is that we are all trapped within language (all of the world is constructed through language) and we acquire our culture through language. We are speaking subjects who operate through the language that structures our thinking. To understand culture, you must understand the structures that function within it, and the underlying patterns that shape it. Everything is structure!

Roland Barthes

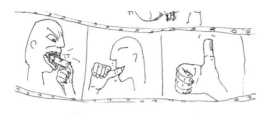

Roland Barthes exemplifies the best of these structuralist readings of culture and society, particularly in the analysis of signs in popular culture. The importance of the mass media in disseminating ideological views of the world is based on its ability to make signs, images, signifiers, work in a particular way, to produce different meanings. Barthes brilliantly discusses the structures that make signs work in particular ways, and shows how myths work in culture.

(A rose is a sign for love, and a raven is a sign of death)

So Barthes analyses the way in which 'signs' (images, words, things) convey deeper, mythical meanings within popular culture (as opposed to the obvious surface meanings of things.) For Barthes the meaning of things comes from how they are placed in the structure and in how it signifies.

The Union Jack signifies the nation, the crown, the empire, "Britishness" etc, etc.

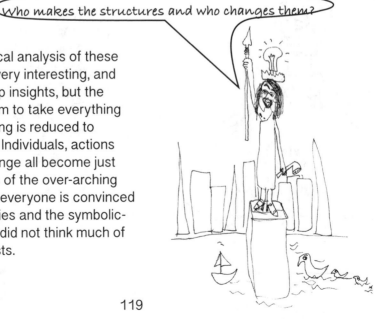

Who makes the structures and who changes them?

The semiological analysis of these 'structures' is very interesting, and produces sharp insights, but the structures seem to take everything over - everything is reduced to the structures. Individuals, actions and social change all become just manifestations of the over-arching structure. Not everyone is convinced by these theories and the symbolic-interactionists did not think much of the structuralists.

Multiple Sociologies

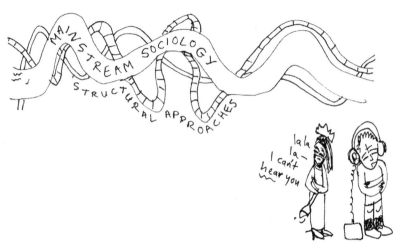

Structuralist approaches to culture and society bypassed mainstream sociology in that they tried to ignore each other. However, in effect, sociology has begun to unravel as a discipline as more and more areas of society, culture and the media have become the sites of study.

There are really many 'sociologies' which reflect the extraordinary complexity of present-day society.

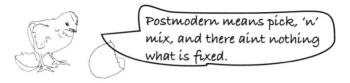

Postmodern means pick, 'n' mix, and there aint nothing what is fixed.

All we can say is that the basic sociological problems like -

Is social structure more important than individual agency?

Or:
Does class still exist?

- are still there.

These questions are approachable from a wide range of theoretical perspectives which seem to reflect what we now call the 'postmodern condition'. We will come back to this later.

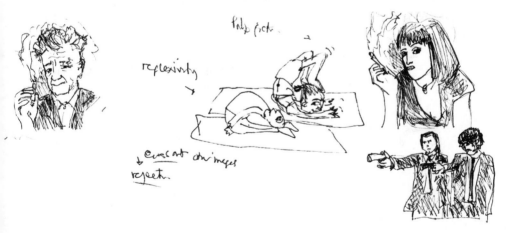

Feminism

The structuralists put themselves forward as a revolutionary change in sociology but the real revolution came from a different quarter.
The approach to traditional sociology (Weber, Durkheim, Merton etc) that most critically undermines its claims to universal truth is that of feminism. From the welfare state to the media, feminists argue that sociology's explanations simply reproduce the idea that gender relations are 'natural' and that women fulfill the social roles that are relevant and appropriate.

An awful lot of sociology simply didn't talk about women at all.

We were invisible, except as the category of "mother".

The classic sociological debates about class are, quite simply, about men and class. If a man is a labourer, then that definition is treated as including the wife, which is not really very scientific.

In politics, discussions of the vote and of political rights were always, in effect, about the male, as discussions of citizenship showed.

What is Feminism?

This a question that preoccupies many people, including sociologists. In present day society there are now very many competing views as to what Feminism is, and in some ways it has become mainstream. In general we can define Feminism as being a critique of society based on the inequalities that exist through gender roles and assumptions. Or, to put it another way, it is women demanding equality in terms of access to education, jobs, income, politics and power. It is a sociological fact that if you are a woman your chances of becoming Prime Minister, or a doctor, a lawyer, or a CEO are much less than if you are a man.

The main feminist critique of sociology can be summed up as:

1) Sociological research has always concentrated on men.
2) The research is then generalized to the whole population.
3) Areas of women's concerns, like reproduction, have been ignored.
4) Value-free research actually means sex-blind research, and women are presented in a distorted manner.
5) Sex and gender are not considered as important variables in analysing the social, whereas they are critical.

Historically it has always been believed that women are not as good as men, although the extent of this belief has varied a lot. It is only in the last fifty years that women have actually achieved anything approaching equality, and it is still a limited achievement. Feminist critiques of society are based on the idea that people are born more or less equal, and that it is the way in which society organizes things that leads to discrimination.

Recently it has become apparent in education that when girls are given the same opportunities as boys they actually do better in almost all subjects.

This is worrying for boys, because they have increasingly limited job opportunities in a world where technology is replacing muscle power as the dynamo of economic production. Traditional models of masculinity are being undermined by these processes.

Sociology's emphasis on industrial society, on work and labour, has always concentrated on what is a male sphere. Now that is changing, because the economy is changing, and sociological debate is beginning to catch up.

Feminist critiques of society undermine the way everything is organized, even sociology itself.

In sociology, the debate about feminism gets very complicated because most sociologists were, and are, men.

The way historical sociologists thought you should do sociological research was very much based on their outlook as men. For example, the whole debate about class – and in which class you belong - was based on looking at what men did, and the women were seen as add-ons. It was as though women didn't exist except as mothers, wives and bolt-on bits of their husbands.

When sociology looked at politics and power, it looked at the public sphere, which is also predominantly male.

The private sphere, the domestic, was always ignored.

The division of labour between male and female and the public and the private was assumed to be 'natural', that is based in biology, and therefore not in need of investigation.

When you consider that sociology was meant to be a 'science of society' it seems odd that something so fundamental was taken for granted. That is not a very scientific attitude.

The programme that feminism would advocate for a reconstructed sociology would look something like this:

1) Placing gender at the heart of all analysis on a par with class and race.

2) Criticizing all sociological theory for its 'male' perspectives, which means analysing the unconscious, as well as conscious, attitudes that structure sociologists' outlook.

3) Analysing the relationship between the public and private spheres as being of central importance in understanding how society functions.

4) Overhauling all of sociological theory.

One of the other outcomes of the feminist critique of sociology was an increasing awareness of the importance of race and anti-racism, which also implied another fundamental criticism of the categories of sociological theory.

Globalization

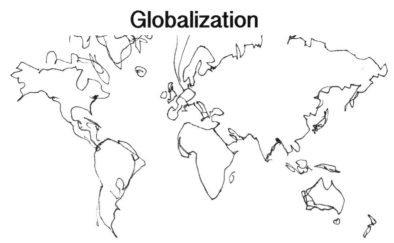

From the certainties of functionalism in the 1950's, the world and sociology have changed a great deal. Since the advent of the internet global society has gone through a massive shift and this has led to a similar transformation in sociology itself. The speed at which society changes has meant that sociology is almost running to keep up with the pace of change.

Sociology's task has been completely redefined both by the undermining of traditional theoretical approaches and by the sudden and rapid transformation of post-war industrialized nation-states into what we can loosely call postmodern global economies. In the space of 20 years whole industries, particularly in places like South Wales, have disappeared, and with them have gone whole ways of life.

Often the women married to miners are the only ones now working. And the work is in high-technology industries, that themselves are coming to redefine the economy and society we operate in. People now ask whether the old working class still exists at all. The last coal mine in Britain closed in December 2015!

Settled patterns of work, education, leisure and domestic life have all been transformed over the last twenty years. Heavy 'manual labour' - classically male jobs - have all but disappeared, and most people now work in front of a computer screen. Many more women work than ever before and everyone has to have digital skills to survive – it is the biggest change in work/life situations that there has ever been.

One of the theoretical problems that contemporary sociology has to deal with, along with the digital revolution, is its historical focus on the nation-state. It has always assumed the nation-state as its natural sphere of analysis. American sociology focused on American society, economy, class, structure and culture, and British sociology did the same for British Society.

Some cross cultural comparisons were made but basically it was assumed that each nation state had its own culture and ways of doing things. Globalization breaks down the nation-state and the culture of postmodernism, of consumerism and celebrity culture, removes the barriers between different states and produces a global society that is increasingly homogeneous. Sociology therefore has to re-think most of the ways it theorizes society. So sociology, cultural studies and media studies tend to blend into a wider discipline in order to theorize things.

Key Features of Globalization

The sociological question is whether this new form of global society is leading to a 'global society' - or is it a contradictory and differential process?

However, the process of the global integration of commerce, media, companies, markets and cultures, and of policy making, is clearly a process that is accelerating. There are global trade agreements that define and control almost all of the world's trading patterns.
The inter-connectedness of almost all economies now means that everyone is in it together.

Now work is in high-technology industries that themselves are coming to redefine the economy and society we operate in.

Michel Foucault

The long standing critique of sociology as being limited by the social and ideological forms and ideas of its time was given greater emphasis by the work of Michel Foucault.

Foucault pointed out that like all other disciplines:

> Sociology is not a value-free discipline, but a discourse about society that influences that society and its ideas about truth.

What Foucault represents is the crisis within sociology in terms of its ability to give a comprehensive picture of society. His main theoretical concerns have centred around how knowledge is produced and utlized in society, and how power and discourse are linked to knowledge. It is a sociology of knowledge in one sense, but it is also a radical deconstruction of the neat disciplinary boundries that sociology has often attempted to construct.

Meta Narrative

Foucault's radicalism is part of what we call the postmodern turn in sociology – what he calls the refusal of all "meta-narratives", or grand theories, about society and history. (A meta-narrative is a grand theory, like Marxism, that tries to explain everything through one theory).

Foucault's work is anti-essentialist, anti-historical and very critical of attempts to argue that something like sociology is "value-free".

The emergence of sociology as a discipline is really bound up with particular descriptions of society, with a form of power in society, an apparatus- the educational and professional structures of sociology – and with the control of certain discourses about society.

- We've come a bit of a way from "social facts" and science, haven't we?

Foucault's most radical work was concerned with sexuality and the body, and the way these are constructed in discourse and social process.

In his hands, sociology becomes an undermining of almost all empirical categories and a re-thinking of what it means to be human. Foucault wants everyone to understand that all human activity is socio-culturally created, not given. His work is unique, complicated and quite controversial.

Jean Baudrillard

Baudrillard is another who drives a stake into the empirical heart of sociology. His view is that society, as some kind of social fact, does not exist. Or if it does, it is entirely composed of signs. This postmodern view sends some sociologists into a frenzy, or a rage, as it is empirically known. What Mr. B. is saying is that our perceptions of society in the digital age, the post-industrial age, are skewed by the nature of the televisual world that we occupy. Real jobs and real industries have been replaced by the internet.

Baudrillard

"Everything is hyperreal, and individuals are just illusions of digital selfreflection."
However the question still remains can you investigate society at all?

What I mean is that televisual communications, and its signs, have so come to dominate global reality that people have a great deal of difficulty deciding what is real.
Therefore, if everybody finds it difficult to understand the real, how can sociologists theoretically pin it down?
We live in a post-infotainment giant-screen Disney meta-world and sociology is about as useful as Egyptian trigonometry would be to an astronaut.

Research Methodology

Whatever theory of society that you have if you are going to investigate society at all then you need some idea of research methods. These are the basic ways in which we go about investigating and explaining how society works. So, having discovered that sociological theories are as numerous as positions in the Karma Sutra, the question is "How do you actually do sociology, rather than theorize about it?"

It should come as no surprise that the different theoretical approaches lead to different methodological approaches (ways of doing research).

If you are going to study society then you first need to think about how you observe and document it. Without empirical evidence – that is data, information, statistics, facts or whatever – you won't get very far. (Although this has never stopped politicians making wild statements about society.)

What you need to be a sociologist:

Some sociological theory.

Some idea of research methods.

A problem to study (Why do women get paid less

A sociological imagination.

Pen and paper.

At least 95% of sociologists woudl agree with that.

A grant to do research.

Somewhere to work.

An idea of how to collect data.

Once you have all of these you are completely ready to start and you just need a computer, preferably a lap-top, because they are cooler. The ability to understand statistics is also vital.

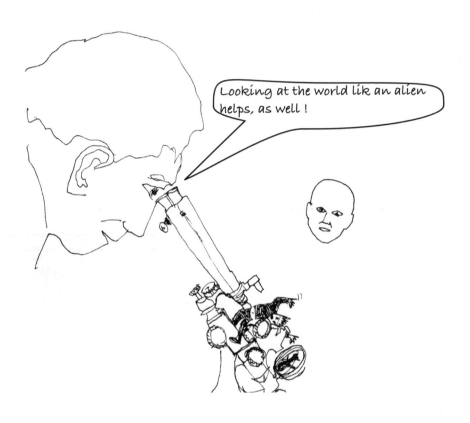

Sources

The most important aspect of doing sociology is the simple question of collecting information.

Where do you get it from?
Off the internet or out of the papers is not a very good answer because these are secondary and unreliable sources. You have to work very hard to find real information - there is a great deal of rumour around and not very many facts.

So what are the key sources?
We divide research into primary and secondary sources, and primary is always best.

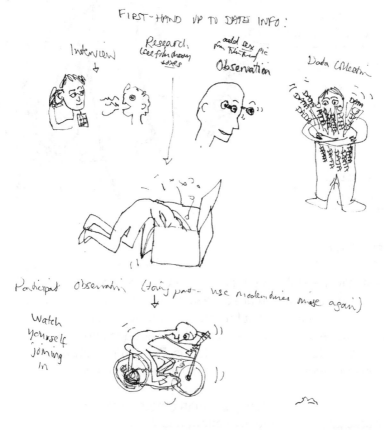

FIRST-HAND UP TO DATE INFO:

Interview

Research,
(see film theory boxes)

added ex pic
from film/ref pic
Observation

Data Collection

Participant observation (doing part-- use middle class more again)

Watch yourself joining in

Primary sources

This is the real McCoy, the first-hand, up to date information produced by you the Sociologist.
This is done through interview, research, observation, data collection or sometimes PO, participant observation (or any other method you can think of). PO is about taking part in things to see how they function.

Social surveys are a very common way of collecting nformation – and the internet does make it easier to do surveys – but you have to think about how reliable the information produced is.

What sort of data do I need and where will I get it from? These are the key questions.

Would you vote for the nasty, vicious Tories or the warm cuddly Labour party? Probably the Labour party

It's too embarrassing to admit I'm a Tory.

Secondary Sources

This is basically the stuff that already exists, the government statistics, previous research, documentaries, newspaper reports, documentary archives, inquiry reports and databases of already existing information. This is information that already exists but you need to know how to analyze it, where it came from and how reliable it is. Research methodology is the way that you go about this process of collecting information.

Some sources are clearly more valid than others! (Many newspapers are seriously unreliable as sources of information!)

Questionnaires

These are the simplest and most straightforward way of trying to find out what people really think about things. Basically you draw up a list of questions and then go and ask people what they think.

You write down what they say, analyze it and then summarize it coming to a general conclusion, which you try and support with your evidence. It sounds pretty simple but it can get quite complicated. You have to get the questions right.

Sociology deals with self-consciousness, thinking interactive people, rather than with chemicals, and therefore gathering information is fraught with prejudice and possible misinterpretation.

If everyone told the truth when asked questions that would help a lot as well, but they don't!

The Hawthorne Effect

(named after somebody
called Hawthorne)

hmmm

AN UNAMBIGUOUS
QUESTION.

When constructing a questionnaire you need to try and make sure that the questions are sensible, that is, they don't lead people into answers they might not mean. The questions have to be unambiguous so that everyone understands them and relevant to what you are trying to discover.
One of the major problems with all questionnaires (or surveys) is that people very much tend to say what they think the interviewer, or other people, expect them to say. The sociologist, like the police officer, has to apply a kind of rational procedure that can ferret out the truth by a combination of insight, thought and evidence. A lot of sociologist's time is spent trying to think up ways of producing hard information, and in then assessing what it means.

The effect of the interviewer or sociologist being in a particular situation and influencing it is known as the Hawthorne effect. (When an official sounding person asks people if they committed crime they tend to say, No!) This came from studies, called the Hawthorne Studies, into behaviour in the workplace during the 1920's and 30's.

Interviews

Another important way to try and find out what people actually think and believe is through interviews. They can be short ones with lots of people, or very long ones with just a few people.

So what is good about interviews? If they are well-structured and conducted with the right sorts of people, they can, through good questions, get a balanced picture. Carefully prepared interviews can give rich, quantifiable data and information.

What are the drawbacks? Interviewer bias, bad questions, people saying the right thing rather than the truth.

How can you avoid this? Say you were interested in children and shop-lifting. If you ask a direct question kids will deny ever shop-lifting. If you ask more general questions about money, jobs, getting a thrill, what kids get up to when they are in gangs, they are more likely to talk about shop-lifting eventually. So interviews need to be thought about and questions organised to get people to talk. Through an interview you can get more depth on the topic, more valid responses and thoughtful discussion. In an in-depth interview (semi-structured) you can get at what people really believe and even things that they haven't thought about before. The danger then is of leading people on in interviews and feeding them ideas, or persuading them to agree to pre-conceived notions.

A greater problem in interviews is people's tendency to exaggerate, to show off and even to lie, particularly about sexual exploits, just to impress the interviewer.

Participant Observation

The ultimate form of long unstructured interviews is participant observation, which means going to live with the group you are interested in. A famous example of this was **John Howard Griffin**, who dyed his skin black and lived as a black man in the southern states of America(1960).

Another famous instance was **Hunter Thompson** who lived with a bunch of Hell's Angels and observed their culture in depth. (1967). He was probably worse than them in terms of delinquent behaviour.

Participant observation came from social anthropology, where practitioners went and lived among the 'primitive' cultures they were studying. Anthropologists look at the culture as a whole, whereas sociologists tend to study smaller groups within complex cultures, particularly in modern societies.

One of the really basic things is that it takes forever.
And you tend to start liking the people you are with. You don't remain sufficiently distanced from those who ran things.

The Statistical Approach

At the other end of the research spectrum some sociologists go for the systematic scientific approach using number crunching, sampling, big data and the quantification of results. Sociology in the internet age has changed considerably since so much data is now available.

Knowledge about what people do, and their shopping preferences for example, has grown exponentially in the last ten years, so that sociology really does have to pay attention to big data and statistical information. The theoretical question is what do we actually do with all this information that can be gathered on the internet?

Statistics and sociology have effectively been re-written in the last ten years. The real question today is all about the accuracy of the statistical information that is gathered.

Constructing social samples and analysing the information you receive in statistical terms is now quite a large part of sociological study.

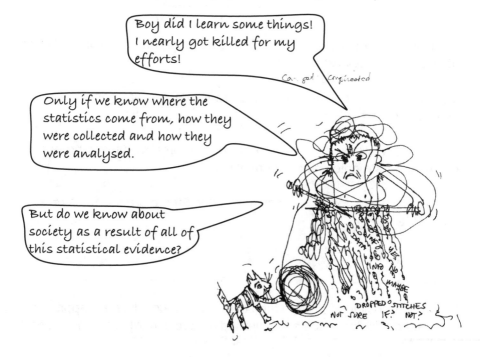

Theory and Methodology

The point about all of these different approaches (or research methods) is that at the end of the day they are all based on what theoretical position you adopt to explain and understand the society you see in front of you. Everyone has a theory of the world, whether they have worked it out or not.

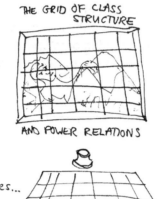

If you are a functionalist like Durkheim , you interpret everything in terms of large-scale social structures.

If you are a symbolic-interactionist, you interpret the way people understand each other.

If you are a Marxist, or a neo-Marxist, you interpret everything through the grid of class struggle and power relations.

If you are a philosopher, you tend to wonder if there are any facts or realities at all.

In practice, sociologists often tend to mix and match different approaches and methodologies, since each method produces particular types of data.

What is Culture ?

CULTURE ?

So to start doing sociology you have to adopt a theoretical position (empiricism or structuralism or symbolic-interactionism etc) and then try and work out a research methodology that fits that theoretical approach. Then the sociologist has to confront a number of problems that make up the key areas of debate in modern sociology. Because society is always changing it means that the way sociology is done also has to change.

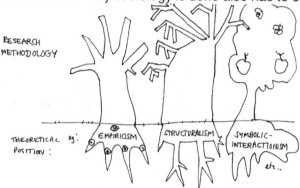

RESEARCH
METHODOLOGY

THEORETICAL eg: EMPIRICISM | STRUCTURALISM | SYMBOLIC-
POSITION : INTERACTIONISM
etc..

One of the most difficult problems that sociologists confront is that of defining CULTURE, one of those words that create endless debates. Here are some working definitions of what the word might mean.
1) The norms, values, ideas and ways of doing things in a particular society. This is the very broad definition of culture.
2) All of the means of communication, art, material things and cultural objects that a society has in common. The cultivation of the mind, the civilization and learning of a society. This is the narrower definition.
3) The ways of life shared by a particular group (e.g working-class culture).
4) The practices that produce meaning in a society (signifying practices) the way culture is organised.
(Do we live in a digital culture these days, and what does that mean?)

The original use of the term 'culture' came from farming and meant the cultivation or development of the land. This grew into a notion of civilized, as opposed to natural, behaviour and came to be used to describe the way in which superior groups (the aristocracy) behaved. A later Enlightenment notion was that all society was developing towards a higher, more complex, culture based on science and rationality. It was at this point that the nature/culture divide began, and led to the idea of the dominance of industrial culture over backward nature.

During the 19th century the idea of "high culture", as the best of art and thought and music, took over and sociologists' approach to the idea of culture became more confused. In the 20th century, popular culture arrived on the scene and made the whole debate even more complicated.

Television culture reduced sociologists simply to analysing the way in which culture in general operated, talking about 'signifying systems' and how we now live in what is called a 'digital' culture.

The Problem of Culture

The problem with trying to understand the 'culture' of a society is that the most general idea of culture – an entire way of life - virtually covers the whole of society. The reason people tend to behave in a particular way, say at weddings, family gatherings or other social events, is that this kind of behaviour is determined by the culture that people live in. So sociologists have to try to refine the idea of culture all the time and even explain what the different 'cultures' are. We can talk about 'popular culture' , 'mass culture', 'high culture', 'lad's culture', and also people who are 'uncultured',

So clearly the definition of culture has to be worked at when one is trying to make sociological statements. Another attempted definition would be something like this: " The use that humans make of symbols, artefacts and communication in order to live a communal life."

The Sociology of Culture

The question of identity, of how people define themselves, and how they develop their identity in culture, is another important aspect of sociology. Contemporary culture defines the key process of socialization (the way that people are brought into society through education, the family and identity), the way in which people develop a sense of self in the digital age.

So culture is really the way that a large group of people do things, built up over time and transmitted from generation to the next. Our culture is a way of behaving that helps people make sense of the world and makes sure everybody knows what they are supposed to be doing. Identity in contemporary culture is something however that seems to be changing rapidly.

Identity gets more and more free-wheeling in the postmodern world, and is easier to redefine, people really can re-invent themselves.

146

Culture and Language

Because culture is such a difficult thing to analyse some sociologists try and ignore it and concentrate on statistics. Culture is such an all-encompassing concept that perhaps it is easier to break it down into bits. The question then becomes What are the elements of 'culture'? We can say that language, ideas, norms, and values and material culture are the elements of culture, and the question is how they inter-relate. Language is the key that distinguishes man from animals and it is the mode in which all culture is communicated and transmitted.

When as a child you acquire language, you also acquire a whole culture. Some sociologists think that language is neutral, but others think it is very significant in shaping the way individuals think. Structuralists argue that the structure of language governs the signifying system of culture.

Some theorists think that language determines culture so that, for example, being Chinese is very bound up with the language itself (this is known as the linguistic-relativity hypothesis.)
The structuralist approach argues for the central importance of language in all theories of culture.

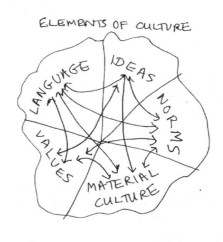

ELEMENTS OF CULTURE

LANGUAGE · IDEAS · NORMS · VALUES · MATERIAL CULTURE

LANGUAGE

Culture and Social Norms

Culture operates through agreed sets of rules called social norms (or codes or mores).

In settled, traditional cultures the social norms are and clear and distinct, for example in the British Christian society of the 19th century. There was a high degree of social conformity and an acceptance of Christian family values as being the basis on which social norms operated.

We could call this British Imperial culture. And if you were white and middle-class it seemed like a very good thing. Everybody knew their place, social etiquette was clear, and the lower orders were very respectful.

In the 20th and 21st centuries there were massive changes in the way that culture was shaped and experienced. This is often understood as being the rise of 'mass culture' , which means that rather than the acceptance of traditional, Christian values the rise of mass newspapers, radio and TV led to the dominance of entertainment, pleasure and secularism. In fact, in the 21st century digital culture the inter-connected world of TV, film and internet has changed everything again.

Mass Culture

'Mass culture', it was claimed, was the product of the industrialization and commercialization of culture, which meant that the newspapers, films, and other cultural products were now produced in a more organized and efficient way with the deliberate aim of making money out of their consumption. Sociologists of the Frankfurt school put forward the argument that this new mass culture was being imposed from above by a new commercial bourgeoisie who recognized the possibilities in a new wage-earning proletariat with disposable income and the desire to be distracted from everyday life.

This argument that mass culture was a kind of opium for the masses is not shared by everyone, and is seen as being pessimistic and simplistic. The Frankfurt School were the biggest supporters of this argument. Others have argued that popular culture is more open and pleasure seeking then previously, and thus more democratic.

Popular culture today, or celebrity culture, is pretty much a global phenomena. There are those who argue that this is not mass culture but "popular culture", and that pop culture is critical of traditional "high culture", and is therefore a good thing.

Class and Stratification

One theme that runs through the debate about popular or mass culture is that of the existence of the rich and the poor. Social stratification (class) seems to exist in all societies, even supposedly equal Communist societies. So how does sociology explain this? Stratification means that different groups in society occupy different places within the pecking order. There are rich and poor, and people in the middle. There are Royal Families and there are homeless people. There are rich farmers and factory workers, and people who work in call centres. Sociologists have long noted that the members of a particular group seem to have common outlooks, similar interests and distinct life styles. People's experience of life tends to be defined by the group, or the place they occupy, in the social order. A key question is that of social mobility - can people move up the social ladder?

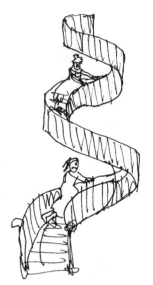

This is what leads sociologists to think that groups are more important in society than individuals.

The functionalists and the social system side argue that stratification is necessary, and the conflict theorists argue that it is the result of an unequal distribution of power and wealth.

Marx argued very clearly that class was the fundamental stratification in society, and that was all there was to say about it.

Explaining Social Inequality

Trying to understand social inequality was put on the map by Karl Marx with his important ideas on class. He had a theory of who exercised power and how they came to have it, through control of the means of production (factories, capital, land, technology etc.) Instead of arguing that poor people were poor because they deserved to be (the feckless masses) he argued that the control of economic resources and wealth defined the class structure. The position you were born into in this class structure then determined the likely outcome of your health, wealth, education, and future occupation. The existence of classes in society is debated a lot today, and some argue that it is no longer relevant.

This poses a number of questions, particularly about how social differentiation works.

What is class?

What is stratification?

What is class mobility ?

Has class disappeared in modern society ?

Everyone says that class doesn't matter now, and yet they've just announced that the "underclass" is the biggest problem in modern society.

What does that mean ?

Marxists argue that class is determined by the relationship to the means of production, and that the consciousness and culture of a class follow from that. Weberians (followers of Max Weber) say that class more reflects an individual's position in the market place. So what Weber said was:

Yes, there are classes in society, but inequality can't be explained just in terms of ownership and property.

In essence, economic relations determine everything else- the cultural, the personal, the law, the entire "superstructure" of what I call ideology.

There are more things to class than just economics, although that is still important.

There are classes, but there is also the problem of status and of parties, and of religion and culture.

The culture of society is the culture of the ruling class.

Marx's model cannot explain the middle-classes who constitute an ever-growing and powerful group.

> Weber said that yes, there are classes in society, but inequality can't be explained just in terms of ownership and property.

> Marx argued that In essence, economic relations determine everything else - the cultural, the personal, the law, the entire "superstructure" of ideology.

> There are classes, but there is also the problem of status and of parties, and of religion and culture.

> The culture of society is the culture of the ruling class. Marx's model cannot explain the middle-classes who constitute an ever- growing and powerful group.

> There are more things to class than just economics, although that is still important.

Does Class Still Matter?

Many politicians now like to claim that class is an out-dated idea and that everyone is equal in a free-enterprise society, but this is highly debateable. How to define class has been a tricky problem and everyone in sociology says that Weber's work is in debate with the ghost of Marx, in the sense that their competing definitions set the tone of the argument. Defining class gets more complicated all the time.

At the end of the day, it is about economic power. However you dress it up, that is what determines people's life chances. " Behind every great fortune there is a great crime"

However, understanding how complex class society has become needs a 20th century viewpoint. Class, status, hierarchy and social position are as much to do with cultural ideas as with straight economic power.

Humbug! the spectre of Communism will wander around till the end of time.

Listen, my special friend, you wrote when industrial society was still being formed. So it was difficult to predict what would happen.

A pair of sociologists known as **Davies and Moore** (1945) argued that stratification existed in all known societies and therefore it must have a functional necessity for society. This nicely meant that the best people always got the top jobs and that there is no such thing as discrimination or power elites. This basically functionalist approach is clearly an exaggeration. Lots of research has demonstrated that elites reproduce themselves by control of access to education and jobs, which are then denied to other people. Discrimination against ethnic groups and women has been so amply demonstrated that there are few people left who still deny it.

These issues bring us to the question of social mobility and of meritocracy, as well as the use of power to control things.

Is an elite maintained in society because members of that elite have greater access to wealth, power, education, contacts and rewards or because they are naturally better at things?

With aristocrats in prison for fraud and drugs, with members of the Royal family behaving like teenagers in a soap opera, one could be forgiven for thinking that being upper-class is coterminous with in-bred stupidity.

So do we have a classless society in which everyone has equal life opportunities?

Is social mobility a reality which means that anyone can become the Queen?

Probably not, but the degree of classlessness in society is hotly debated.

Do elites still exist? Many sociologists argue that class is no longer a significant factor, but others argue that despite having changed, the existence of class is still a significant factor in the functioning of culture, particularly in Britain. So contemporary sociology has to think carefully about identity, class and how people perceive themselves.

So why do so many people in Britain identify themselves by class?

Is class defined by wealth, by education, or by hereditary principles?

Why do children from the manual working classes, as we used to define them, do so badly in education and jobs?

Why are the sons and daughters of the professional middle-classes over-represented in the elite universities?

Who do people keep saying that class has disappeared?

The Underclass

Just when it felt safe to be 'de-classed', sociologists decided that the new problem was the underclass. Over the last twenty years many traditional working-class jobs have disappeared, mainly because of new technology and machines, and this has produced a new group of people who, through lack of skills, wealth, property or education, appear to be virtually outside society. The underclass really means the people who are superfluous in a globlized economy where production can be moved around the world to the cheapest place, often the developing nations and China. (This group is now often targeted as benefit scroungers.)

So the unskilled in the advanced capitalist countries are replaced by cheap labour in the developing world, like China, or by technology.

The unemployed are always blamed for being unemployed, and then social scientists like Charles Murray come along with their theories of the underclass and say that it exists because the state gives them "too much money".

Charles Murray reckons that if you give people welfare benefits, they become 'dependent' on them and then they don't want to work, and hey presto, you have an underclass. In America and in the UK the argument from the neo-liberal wing has become that you have to take benefits of people and 'encourage' them back into work.

The problem of jobs, wage levels and training and skills is often left out of this discussion- but for the sociologist the question is how to understand and define these groups.

There is another group in the UK now known as NEETS - this is young people not in education, employment or training, who are therefore also almost outside the system.

As the Office of National statistics put it last year (2014) There were 963,000 young people (aged from 16 to 24) in the UK who were Not in Education, Employment or Training (NEET), an increase of 9,000 on July to September 2014 and down 78,000 from a year earlier.
This is a lot of people and an interesting sociological problem.

Welfare and Poverty

These problems of the underclass raise the whole question of wealth, poverty and the 21st century phenomenon of the welfare state. What has become very clear in the last decade is that the gap between the rich and the poor has not been disappearing but in fact has been widening. So this question of "Why are people poor" leads to very interesting debates about what the function of the welfare state is.

Sir William Beveridge (1879-1963) was the Director of the London School of Economics and the inventor of the Welfare state after the second World-war. Its aim was to provide for those who, through no fault of their own, were unemployed, ill, old, or simply poor. This social democratic idea sounds very reasonable, but many Conservatives opposed it then, and even more so do now.

There is a constant barrage of denunciation, and television exposure, of the 'life on Benefits' brigade, who are regularly demonised and attacked.

Society today is very much bound up with the arguments about the welfare state. Market liberals strongly argue that the welfare state interferes with individual freedoms (it helps people). At one level it is a debate about how society should work. Should it be completely capitalist or does the community come first?

Should 'society' still look after everybody is the real question.

Beveridge's welfare state was based on essentially liberal ideas of what it meant to a 'citizen', to be part of a caring society in which people had equal rights. This modern idea of the nation-state is really one of a community of citizens who all have common rights and freedoms. These ideas of rights and freedoms constantly come up against the realities of economic power, ownership and access to educational and political power. The neo-liberal orthodoxy that exists today rejects many of the social-democratic ideas of rights and insists instead on the idea of competition and of the state not supporting welfare. The questions of identity and socialization, how and why people reproduce the culture of their parents, has also become an important issue here, some studies looking at three generations of unemployed people living on benefits.

My ideas about the post-war welfare state were meant to cement the relationship between "citizenship" and "welfare", and to enshrine the rights of individuals to health, employment

From its very inception, we Conservatives have attacked the idea of the welfare state as being an infringement on the free play of market forces, which we claim really dictate how societies function.

On one side the social –democratic arguments (which do derive from an era when there seemed to be full-employment and no suggestion that it would not continue.)

In the other corner the arguments of the neo-liberals, the new right.

The Two Arguments

Market forces are destructive and uncontrolled.
Capitalism leads to social inequality and lack of welfare.
Capitalism produces disharmony, lack of consensus and, as in the 1930's, can ultimately lead to war.
Capitalism should not be hampered by the state. The market should decide everything.
Government breeds bureaucracy which stifles the production of wealth.
State planning, welfare and organization are always more inefficient than the free market.
Individuals should look after themselves and the state should not intervene.
The welfare state makes people dependent on it, and is therefore a bad thing.

These arguments within sociology - and social policy - have become much more marked in the 21st century, and sociology itself has been under attack by the neo-liberals within the academic world. The free-market neo-liberal ideology that the market should determine everything and that the state should not intervene has become the dominant ideology in Britain and America, In fact education, welfare, health services and many other things have been 'privatized' in the last decades and this has fundamentally changed both society and the way in which it is perceived.

This has been a long extended attack on the ideas of the welfare state and a re-writing of the idea of the importance of society. There is much more emphasis now on the 'individual' and on how they should be responsible for themselves.
Welfare is now seen as almost a moral aberration that needs to be controlled and regulated by the functions of the free-market. Identity is no longer a responsibility of the state, but of the private individual.

Free-marketers regularly attack the whole idea of sociology, claiming that society is not an observable entity.

What about the family?

Oddly enough, the free-marketers also claim that the family is a vital unit in society and often claim that it is disintegrating and needs to be supported. Why this traditional form of organisation needs to be retained unlike all of the other forms of social organisation probably relates to the way in which the family plays such a key role in socialization and in maintaining the status quo. That is why the Royal family are so useful, they are the paradigm of tradition and 'normal' family life.

From functionalists to postmodernists, everyone has some kind of argument about what role the family plays in society, and why.

The absolutely central question is whether or not the family is a universal institution in all societies, and to what extent does the way it is organized, vary?

Or to put it another way, where do gender roles come from ?
Does the family reproduce them and is the family natural, unnatural, an agent of capitalism or necessary for individuals to survide in society?

In Asian society, the family is often overtly the model for the whole of society.

162

As this is a family book we'll have a polite quiz on these questions to keep everyone amused. The trick is to identify the different theoretical approaches to understanding the role of the family.

The All-Time Family Quiz

Who invented the family and why?

- ☐ God – for procreation. It's a natural extension of our animal nature and the need to bring up offspring.
- ☐ Man invented it to enslave women and sustain patriarchy.
- ☐ It developed as a social institution out of kinship patterns which included marriage.
- ☐ You're all wrong. Nobody invented it, it just happened.

Who described the modern family as the "cereal-packet norm family?

- ☐ God
- ☐ Mrs Thatcher
- ☐ Ronaldo
- ☐ Edmund Leach – the anthropologist in 1957.

And for ten bonus points what did he mean?

That the 1950's idea of the small nuclear family of Mum, Dad and two Kids was advertised as the norm to which everyone should aspire.

What is wrong with the family?

- ☐ It is conformist and oppressive of women,
- ☐ It reproduces male control of women and children.
- ☐ It allows child-sex abuse to continue unchecked.
- ☐ It legitimizes violence towards women.
- ☐ Nothing at all.

Which sociologist described families as "factories which produce human personalities?

- ☐ Michael Johnson
- ☐ Justin Bieber
- ☐ Edmund Leach
- ☐ Talcott Parsons – the American functionalist writer

And for ten bonus points each, what does he mean and what is a functionalist?

He means that bringing up baby and allowing adults to function in the nasty world of work and competition requires that the family act as a kind of refuge from the outside and allow people's personalities to develop.

A functionalist is someone who thinks that everything in a society, like the family, has a function, a role in making society work.

Which sociologist described the family as an "ideological conditioning device in an exploitative society"?

- ☐ Madonna
- ☐ Talcott Parsons
- ☐ Edmund Leach
- ☐ David Cooper- in The Death of the Family (1970).

And for ten extra points what did he mean?

- ☐ God only knows
- ☐ Something not very nice
- ☐ That the family is the place where children are socialized into conforming to society's rules which are made up by the people who run things.
- ☐ Is he a left-functionalist?

How do you define the family?

- ☐ Mum, dad and two kids who watch television together.
- ☐ An outmoded form of social expression that leads to the exploitation of women and the abuse of children?
- ☐ The loving heart of God's faith and the true sanctity of marriage?
- ☐ A nice idea if you can make it work. Even the Royal family don't seem to be able to make it work.
- ☐ Something that is changing very rapidly in the 21st century.

The family is so important in sociology simply because that is where society is reproduced in its most basic form, the individual. Wherever you start in sociology you have to have some idea of how to conceptualise the family, how it changes and what the connection between the family and society is.

If you look at contemporary China you can see that the family is controlled by society, for many years there was a one-child policy, which has just been relaxed so that people can now have two children!

Socialization

Obviously the family plays a key role in socialization (the way in which individuals are socialized – brought into- society) in fact without the family it is difficult to see how this rearing of individuals could happen. Society reproduces itself through the individuals who themselves are taught the rules of society- the transmission of culture and society. Each part of the socialization process receives different emphasis by different kinds of sociologists.

Freudians think the early years are crucial, some think the family is central, others argue that education is the critical phase.

For a long time education has received sociological attention as being the main force that reproduces the culture and ideas of a society.

Understanding the importance of education in this process of socialization is emphasised differently by different theorists, but it is clearly important.

Whether the family is more important or not is hotly debated. What is referred to as a " culture of benefits" is often seen as being the product of a particular form of socialization within dysfunctional families.

What is Socialization?

Socialization is the process by which children and adults learn from others. It is the way in which a new infant is introduced to, and becomes a part of, society. One begins learning from others during the early days of life; and most people continue their social learning all through life. The early years of socialization are clearly the most important when children acquire language, social skills, ideas of morality and a basic emotional structure of feeling about how to behave.

It's also about the nature/nuture debate – is our behaviour biological or is it determined by the way that we are socialized?

Most sociologists think that the process of socialization is the dominant factor in how individuals turn out.

Really socialization is a process of copying, of imitating the ways of behaviour that adults demonstrate to children.

I hate teaching!

The Sociology of Education

So if parental influence is an important feature of shaping what people become then education comes a very close second. Some people think education is the most important factor but that ignores all of the sociological and physcological
evidence on the shaping power of the early years on the developing infant.

What is education for?

Is it to pass on the culture and values of society to the young? To prepare people for the adult world of work? To educate children about the culture they live in?
To reproduce the class system and to teach people their place in life? To give employment to a lot of people who aren't very good at anything except teaching? To keep kids off the streets until they're old enough to be unemployed? To create a skilled work-force for the economy?

Access to education has historically been rather limited, and until the 20th century most of the lower classes had very limited access to education. In fact mass education is a very new thing historically, and has only been widespread since the Second World War. Before that, serious education was the preserve of the wealthy and then the middle-classes. Even when mass education was introduced working-class students tended to do worse then their middle-class colleagues. (This is probably to do with socialization in which different classes give different emphasis to the importance of education.)

This raises the sociological question of influences and effects.

Is it because working-class children are less intelligent than middle-class children? And, by extension, are different races of different intelligence, as some socio-biologists argue? Or are different educational outcomes to do with the structure, ideas and forms of organization in education? Is education organised to benefit elites?

In a famous book that sums up these debates. **Learning to Labour: How Working-class kids get working class jobs.** (1977) **Paul Willis** looked at the way in which working-class boys in particular rejected the middle-class values of school and thus condemned themselves to working-class jobs. The recent rise of NEETS (not in employment training or education) continues this tradition of white working-class boys refusing to take part in the educational system.

Althusser

The French Marxist and social theorist **Louis Althusser** (1918-90) argued, rather like Gramsci, that education played an important role on spreading bourgeois ideology, or reproducing the dominant culture. This is the strong version of the argument that socialization occurs through the education system and that it is the dominant form that ensures conformity and coherence. Most sociologists agree that education does reproduce the dominant culture, but they differ about its role in the overall process.

Althusser is quite certain that it is profoundly ideological.

The sociology of education then demands analysis of the structures of education, what is taught, who teaches it to whom, and what outcomes this has for the functioning of society.

Class, language, gender, race and intelligence all become key issues in trying to link educational processes to the way people end up perceiving themselves, and therefore acting in society.

Althusser also argued that the mass media were an important means of ideological control in modern society (as do many Marxists and cultural critics) and one of the primary definers of our culture today. There are many contemporary sociologists who argue that the mass media, and particularly digital media, TV and film, influence the process of socialization as much as the family or school. If this argument is correct then it begs a lot questions about how we do sociology today.

The internet is probably the most powerful tool of cultural domination that there has ever been.

Traditional sociology has not really taken that much notice of the mass media, despite the fact that television has clearly changed the whole culture of industrialized countries. Television has utterly changed the way politics is conducted, and has changed out leisure culture from being a public, communal culture into a home based private culture.

If Abraham Lincoln were alive today he would never be elected? He's far too ugly to appear on television.

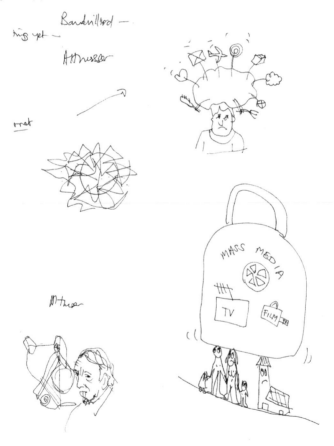

Postmodern Hyperreality

We mentioned Jean Baudrillard earlier, who argued that we live in such a media −saturated society that the culture is now 'hyperreal'. That is to say that the way in which people understand the world is mediated through the digital that there are mostly just simulations that people take for the real. This is a million miles, sociologically speaking, from empirical analysis, social facts and class analysis. If Baudrillard is right, then most sociology can pack up and go home, because looking at social facts will tell you nothing about the psychological dimension in which popular/celebrity culture is so dominant.

Baudrillard does, however, suggest that in some ways people have greater freedom in this postmodern world to pick whatever images and lifestyles they like, which can sound positive.
The jury is still out on the postmodern debate, and some people argue that it is itself just a simulation of a theory.
Television is about a real as watching a goldfish bowl and thinking that is what the sea is like.

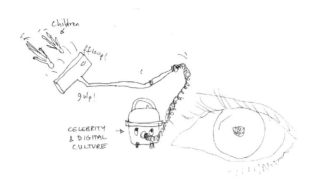

In Baudrillard's approach clearly socialization is dominated by the impacts of the media, and his writing was really at the beginning of the internet age, so that in some senses it has been very prescient. Celebrity culture has grown to be a universal phenomena and the ways that children are now drawn into celebrity and digital culture are much discussed. There is a kind of emotional socialization which takes place through social media and lives, and identities seem to be formed by the influence of social media. The 'hyperreal' of the internet has, it is argued in the last ten years, become the most powerful defining mechanism of contemporary identity and self-awareness.

People live through the X-factor and Gogglebox - the audience becomes the actors.

How one analyses this is really a difficult question for contemporary sociology.

I once said Disneyland is more real than the rest of America.

Television and Crime

Another area in which television, the internet and society meet up is in the representations of crime and deviance. Old fashioned sociology used to talk about the 'criminal mind' or the 'criminal personality' or even the 'criminal classes'. Now television sets the agenda for how people perceive crime and criminality. People's fear of crime is now as important as the facts of crime.

In the 1950's criminals were simply deviants who broke the law. Then in the 1960's sociologists began to talk about "sub-cultures" and "labelling theory" – how people came to be labelled and then acted as criminals.

In another important book, **Policing The Crisis** (1973) a group of sociologists examined the way in which the media began to report and exaggerate crime, in particular, mugging. They then examined how this sort of 'moral panic' spread throughout society and transformed everyone's ideas about crime. In the last two decades the media have taken up crime as sexy, threatening, exciting and great for pulling audiences. There are about thirty serial killers a week on TV.

Sociology and Criminology

Sociology has a long history of discussing crime in society, from Durkheim on suicide to classic studies of gangs in Chicago. Debates about the causes of crime and deviance are very important, but if the media now totally control social ideas about crime, then we are in a wholly different paradigm. Policing the Crisis examined the ways in which the media portrayed certain crimes, like mugging, as 'black crimes' - and this link to racism has become very important in sociological theory. The present situation in the USA in respect of "Black Lives matter" is a clear example of the cultural battle over representations of crime.

The importance of this analysis was that it looked at the creation of stereotypes in the media that relied on unconscious associations rather than overt facts.

The power of these images to shape ideas about crime, race and society does suggest that we now live in a different kind of society in which the media, in little understood ways, constantly reshape culture.

Youth culture is particularly dominated by popular media images, and this impacts on education, fashion, identity and individual self-image. How people come to see themselves, what they see as their identity, is another key issue.

Ever since **Pulp Fiction,** crime and the media have had an oddly friendly relationship.

Contemporary Identity

The question of self-identity, of how people perceive themselves and of how they express that self-conception, is a question that comes out of the rapidly changing nature of society, and of individual's relationships to that society. Who am I? is a battle, a challenge and a process that all individuals go through and which in part, is defined by their relationship to society. So an individual's sense of self – comes out of their gender, race, ethnicity, sexuality, religion and in the ways that these are developed and passed on through the family and education. We are located by our identity and the struggle to form and define it can either be simple, as in some societies where there is a close knit transmission of culture, as in fixed cultures like the Amish, or the ultra-orthodox Hassidim, or very traditional Muslim cultures. The problem of identity is more complex in modern societies where culture is much more fluid, and possible identities develop rapidly. Feminism has importantly transformed the idea of identity in the last seventy years.

How fixed are identities?

This is quite a tricky sociological problem that also relates to gender. It used to be thought it was simple to say he is a man and she is a woman and that is their primary identity (what you are born with, as it were). The odd notions that people used to have about women, and what they could, or could not do, show how even these ideas about identity were based in assumptions rather than facts. Biology is not destiny in the way that traditional thought had it, and just as we are likely to get a woman president of America quite soon, how this changed and how identity gets re-defined is a sociological question.

So the primary identity (gender, family, religion) is more or less defined in the process of socialization, being trained to live in society, but is not actually that fixed. Secondary identity, or the roles or self-identity that individuals choose to develop, is even less fixed and determined. We can choose to become an engineer, a novelist an actor, a gay person, or bi-sexual or, within the constraints of society, almost any kind of person that we want to be.

How and in what way these constraints operate and limit identity is in itself an important question for contemporary society, and the idea of cyborg identity, part-human part machine, shows how far the ideas have developed.

Identity is not therefore as fixed as people in the nineteenth century believed, but is fluid and changing. It is more of a narrative than a given definition. People develop and re-write their identity as they go along.

"Tune in, turn on and drop out" was the call in the 1960's to abandon society and have a new identity. This is where many of the changes in identity began.

In thinking about how identity is constructed and understood in contemporary society the sociologist **Anthony Giddens** has written a lot about it. He argues that in the post-traditional order, a society where culture is no longer based in tradition but in ever changing digital cultures, self-identity becomes a reflexive project – it is a narrative we make up ourselves.

He argues that it is a process that we continuously work and reflect on, we strive to become the person we want to be. In other words we create, maintain and constantly revise a set of biographical narratives - the story of who we are now, how we came to be where we are now and what might happen next.

So in contemporary society self-identity is not just a set of fixed traits or obvious characteristics. Giddens argues that it is in fact a person's own self-reflexive understanding of their biography that defines identity.

I wald say.

Self-identity does have a continuity - that is, it cannot easily be simply changed at will - but that continuity is only a consequence of the person's reflexive beliefs about their own biography. It is about how they think of themselves as the story of their own life. Sometimes this is conducted on Facebook and can be partially imaginary. We tell ourselves a 'story' about our identity.

The definers of identity

Family, class and religion play important parts in defining identity and, despite arguments to the contrary, class and family still play an important role in contemporary British society. One of the questions in today's sociology is exactly how a culture based in celebrity and popular culture obscures the underlying facts of class, religion and family. The idea that anyone can be anything they want to be is a basic ideological premise of this kind of culture, but the evidence is quite different.

The recent rise of endless TV programmes about life on benefits demonstrates quite clearly that these families are seen as being outside the system and to have almost made 'choices' to life on benefits. Whether this is true or not is a difficult sociological question about the formation of identity in contemporary society The relationship between 'personal' identity' and 'social' identity is a question about power and social stratification, and the old 'underclass' have become the new outcasts in the portrayal of benefit culture.

This type of reality TV is sometimes described as poverty porn, and the questions about social power, employment and access to education and training are simply ignored by concentrating on individuals.

The Precariat
(a new social class?)

PRECARIAT

The idea of the freedom to choose one's identity implies that jobs, education and opportunities are available to all, but the recent changes in the nature of how capitalist society is organised shows a very different picture. The impact of new technology over the last two decades has been immense and millions of jobs have been replaced by machinery, leading to both mass unemployment, and to a lack of security in the job market. Wages are driven down and jobs are routinely changed and down-graded so that people do not have any security of employment, as they used to. This is what leads to the argument that there is an emerging new social class, the Precariat. (Precarious and proletarian!).

Guy Standing

A British economist called **Guy Standing** has analysed the precariat as a new emerging social class in his important book **Precariat: The New Dangerous Class** (2011). This particularly applies to younger people today in situations where, despite having education, there are simply no jobs, or there are only part-time badly paid jobs with no security. This leads to financial, social and identity insecurity as people become disaffected and rootless.

(Youth unemployment in Greece is presently 51.80 %).

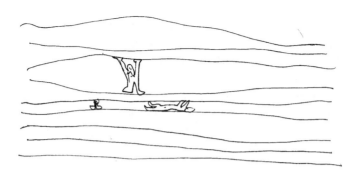

So rather than just thinking about identity, the present questions in sociology are about social stratification and how people are organised in society. Talking about stratification means thinking about the positions that people occupy in society and, like the Precariat, how these positions define what social chances people have in society.

The ability to change your social status, social mobility, to gain education, training, skills, and to better your life chances is an important aspect of social stratification. Much evidence today suggest that social mobility has stalled in many countries and that life chances of young people are more restricted than they were in the 20th century.

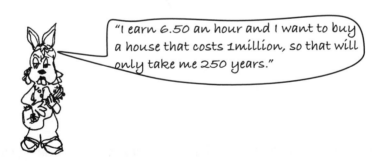

"I earn 6.50 an hour and I want to buy a house that costs 1million, so that will only take me 250 years."

How equal a society is relates to exactly how much social mobility exists in the access to power, education and jobs.

(Is stratification a natural process in all societies? Can it be changed?)

Actually, being a member of the Precariat, a term that still needs more clarification, is a lot worse than being a member of the traditional working-class was - at least they had had stable jobs in the 20th century.

Living in a world that is completely dominated by celebrity culture and the world of social media, it is easy for people to lose themselves in a narcissistic fantasy of excitement that blocks out the real world.

-and that is another difficult question that sociology has to deal with; how do we define the nature of contemporary culture and what sort of theories are applicable today?

The consensus with which sociology started in the 19th century, the idea of a positive, rational science and of objectivity and neutrality, now look like many other 19th century views - cumbersome, grandiose and slightly ridiculous.

Above all else, it is clear that sociology is a product of its time and reflects the ideas and interests of the social groups who control it. What began as a critical social theory, as almost a philosophical enterprise to understand society and man, has ended in a profession that tries to justify its status and objectives by claiming to be a science — or what Michel Foucault calls a discourse - in order to shore up the creaking 19th century edifice.

Sociology has had to theoretically come to terms in the last two decades with the rise of a critical feminism, a re-evaluation of the ways in which sociology itself has thought about men as being naturally more important and also with the very white, European (ethno-centric) approach which lies at the heart of traditional sociology. The critique of imperialism and racism which links the western world's development to the under-development of the third-world has also impacted on how sociology thinks about how things work.

In the face of the massive changes discussed above we can ask: Is Sociology dead?

Is sociology dead?

Is sociology dead?

As a grand set of theories that explain everything in a scientific way, probably yes.

As an impulse to develop a critique of globilization, of the way in which wealth inequality has increased massively in the last decades, and of the ways that global media companies control the spread of celebrity culture, then the answer is no, it is more relevant than ever.

An impulse

Of course since 9/11 the world has also changed dramatically in terms of cultural wars, opposing cultures and religions and in the decline of the Western world as the moral policeman of the world.

Postmodern global culture is everywhere and even national identities are seen as being under threat, and being redefined by globilization. When you add wars on terrorism, global refugee migrations and climate change as well, you can see that sociology faces many more complicated problems than it did in the 20th century – so it is about re-thinking the whole of sociology all over again.

Sociology has therefore to become a critical, political activity as well as an academic activity.

It also has to recognise that almost every area of society it considers is now represented, transformed and shaped by a global culture that pays little attention to old boundaries.

We are probably all going to be urban creatures by the middle of the next century, and that is a strange reality.

Sociology is a generic name for all of the approaches to understanding human behaviour in its modern inter-social forms. Sociology has changed so much in the last twenty years that all sociology is immediately out-dated. However, it is true to say that Sociology has learnt to run faster, and develop new theories - which is quite exciting.

The social question of how technology is re-shaping work, and destroying jobs, is clearly now a burning question.

The question of climate-change, and the impacts of industry on the environment, are also key.

- and the terrible question of terrorism hangs over contemporary society too.

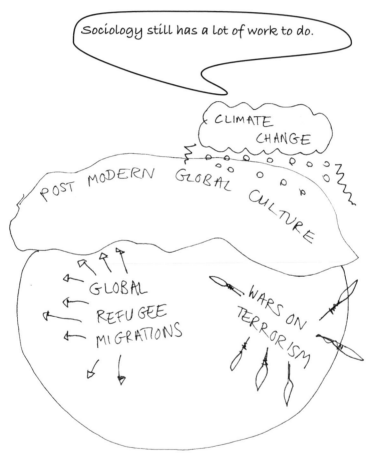

The End.

AQA A Level Sociology Book One Including AS Level Paperback – 22 May 2015-
Rob Webb (Author), Hal Westergaard

Blumer, Herbert 1986 Symbolic Interactionism. Berkeley and Los Angeles:
University of California Press.

Crowley, H. Knowing Women: Feminism and Knowledge (1992) (Open University's
Issues in Women's Studies)

Delamont, S. Feminist Sociology (2009) (BSA New Horizons in Sociology) Sage,
London.

Fulcher, J. and J. Scott (2007) Sociology, Oxford: Oxford University Press.

Garfinkel, Harold 1967. Studies in Ethnomethodology. Oxford: Blackwell Publishers.

Giddens, A. Sutton, P.W. Sociology. (2013) (7th ed) Polity Press

.Habermas, Jrgen (1989.) Theory of Communicative Action. Boston: Beacon Press.

Haralambos and Holborn - Sociology Themes and Perspectives Student Handbook:
AS and A2 level Paperback – 20 May 2013.

Hedstrም, Peter and Peter Bearman (eds.) 2009. The Oxford Handbook of
Analytical Sociology. Oxford: Oxford University Press.

Holborn, M. Contemporary Sociology. (2013)Polity Press. London.

Longhurst, B & Smith, G. Introducing Cultural Studies (2008) Routledge. London.

Macionis, J. and K. Plummer (2011) (5th edition) Sociology: a global introduction,
Harlow: Prentice Hall.

Mills, C.W. The Sociological Imagination. Oxford University Press.1959.

Mead, George Herbert (1967). Works of George Herbert Mead. Vol. 1: Mind, Self,
and Society. Chicago: University of Chicago Press.

Nicholl, F. Gambling in Everyday Life (Routledge Research in Cultural and Media
Studies) 2017.

Swingewood, A. short history of Sociological thought.(1964) Macmillan.

Turner, B.S. The New Blackwell Companion to Social Theory,(2013) Oxford: Wiley
Blackwell.

Turner, B and Rojek, Forget Baudrillard?(1993) Routledge.

Weber, M. The Protestant Ethic and the Rise of Capitalism. (1980) Simon &
Schuster.

Use the Internet – start with the British Sociological Association website – plenty
of information.